The Dance of Dynamic Peace

Lee & Amy,
May you always
be at peace
— Porterfield

Wayne Porterfield

The Dance of Dynamic Peace
Copyright © 2019 by Wayne Porterfield

All rights reserved. No part of this publication may be reproduced, distributed, or transmitted in any form or by any means, including photocopying, recording, or other electronic or mechanical methods, without the prior written permission of the author, except in the case of brief quotations embodied in critical reviews and certain other non-commercial uses permitted by copyright law.

Tellwell Talent
www.tellwell.ca

ISBN
978-0-2288-1381-1 (Hardcover)
978-0-2288-1380-4 (Paperback)
978-0-2288-1382-8 (eBook)

Dedication

This book is dedicated to all of humanity in the proliferation of peace for all living beings. May we always see our interconnectedness with all manifested phenomenon.

May all living beings be at peace.
May we act with compassion, kindness and benevolence.
May we know and cause no harm.
May we spread only peace and love.

Table of Contents

Dedication iii
Preface vii
Introduction ix

Chapter One: Why does peace matter? 1
   Our approach to life 2
   Living in greater harmony 10
   Being open and receptive 14
   Our impact 17

Chapter Two: The dance of dynamic peace 20
   What is inner peace? 21
   The dance 26
   Experiential knowing 29

Chapter Three: Meditation 34
   What is meditation? 35
   Why meditate? 44
   Fostering a regular meditative practice 54
   Meditative practice 63
   Meditation techniques 70
   Being present 79

Guidelines for Establishing
   a Meditative Practice 85

Chapter Four: Creating peace in our life 88
   Do no harm 89
   Consumption 98
   Edible Foods 98
   Sense impressions 107
   Volition 114
   Consciousness 119

Chapter Five: Exploring Self 128
   Judgemental mind 129
   Desire 137
   Passion 144
   The mirror 150
   Kindness 158
   Compassion 164
   Gratitude 170
   Unconditional love 175

Chapter Six: The ripple effects of peace 181
   The pebble in the pond 182
   The Present moment 188
   Family 193
   Community 199
   Global 204

Chapter Seven: Looking forward 209

Acknowledgements 211

Appendix A – Personal Values Exercise 212

Preface

From as far back as I can remember, I have felt ubiquitous fear and anxiety. No single event, that I can recall, has brought about the thoughts and feelings surrounding my fear, though maybe it was a result of having to leave the hospital early, at the time of my birth, due to an outbreak of dysentery in the nursery. Yet, I feel as though fear and anxiety were part of my inherent programming: the predisposition that I came into this world with to experience and transform during my lifetime.

My life has been filled with periods of highs and lows; seldom have I experienced contentment or peace. At times, fear and anxiety have consumed my thoughts, leaving me to worry obsessively. Primarily, my worry has been in regards to suffering and death. The hardships of illness, the atrocities of war, and the loss of a sense of comfort and security were particular areas of fearfulness for me.

A saving grace was when my parents enrolled me in dance classes in a desperate effort to help me release some of my heightened energy. For the first time in my life, I was able to let go of my future-focused, fearful, and anxious self and just be present in the movement. It was bliss. It was also, I believe, my first introduction to a meditative experience.

The next stage of my journey took place around the time my first daughter was born over 30 years ago. I was drawn to explore meditation and periods of deep self-reflection, along with vegetarianism, comparative religion and mysticism. Then, in the 1990s, I spent five years in intense meditation study under the guidance of a spiritual teacher with roots in the Vedic tradition, while living in his sanctuary in Virginia, USA. For the last few years, I have explored Buddhist philosophy and meditation techniques, as well as becoming a student and teacher of yoga.

Through a committed willingness to continually look at myself truthfully with acceptance and love, I have learned to be more at peace within myself and to foster greater peace and joy in my life. My fears and anxieties have softened. I have become more disciplined and self-confident. However, the journey continues. I still experience moments of anxiety to this day, and I know my struggles are not unique. So many people experience pervasive fear and anxiety. We are increasingly overwhelmed with information, technology, the demands of home and work and the failure of societal norms to bring about greater joy and contentment in our lives.

Introduction

When we are able to relax and let go of our suffering, worries and fears, peace reveals itself to us. It is available in each moment, whenever we are still and present enough to notice. As you read through this book, we will explore what is meant by the dance of dynamic peace and look at ways to create greater inner peace in your life.

I will introduce the practice of meditation as a foundation for creating inner peace. Becoming aware of what we consume through food, our senses, volition, and consciousness also contributes to our sense of peace, so we will consider ways in which we can avoid causing harm to ourselves and other beings. To provide you with further insights about creating inner peace, we will explore our judgemental mind, as well as our desires, passions, duality and non-duality, kindness, compassion, gratitude and love. Finally, we will consider the ripple effect of creating a more peaceful and joyous life not only for ourselves but for our families, communities and the larger global community.

At the end of each section, I offer you ideas of how you can apply what you have learned. Some of these practical suggestions are easy to implement while others may be more challenging, so I have grouped them into three levels:

Take a step (easy), Test the waters (more challenging) and Jump in with both feet (the most challenging).

My intention in writing this book is to share what I have learned and experienced in the hope that it will, in some way, be a benefit to you in creating greater peace in your life and ultimately lead to greater peace in the world. I hope you enjoy reading it and sharing it with others you think would also benefit from reading it.

My wish for you is that these words begin to resonate in your consciousness:

May I have peace in my thoughts,
May I have peace in my words,
May I have peace in my heart.
~ Unknown

Chapter One: Why does peace matter?

Know the Power that is Peace.

~Black Elk

Our approach to life

> *It is not impermanence that makes us suffer.*
> *What makes us suffer is wanting things to*
> *be permanent when they are not.*
> ~ Thich Nhat Hanh

In today's industrialized countries, we are dealing with an ever-increasing pace of life, high demands at work and home and the need to be continuously multitasking. Our personal stress levels continue to grow, leading to an increase in ever-present anxiety, depression, and fatigue. The use of opioids and other hallucinogens to escape the pressures of everyday life has increased significantly. But true happiness comes only from within. Rather than seeking to escape our lives, we need to look inward to find peace and contentment.

The world in which we live today is more complex and stressful than any generation before us has experienced. The rate at which we are subjected to information, technological change and business dealings has increased from just five, ten or twenty years ago. Today, we have access to information instantly from around the world as it happens. The news is reported twenty-four hours a day on the internet, radio and television. We can find information on any subject on our computers and mobile devices anywhere in the world at any time of day. We are bombarded daily with information, advertisements and messages that we somehow have to assimilate. Additionally, technological advancements are far outpacing our ability to deal with the social and psychological implications such changes bring.

Consider the advances made in artificial intelligence over the past few years. There are so many ethical questions about its application and use that we as a society have not yet addressed, such as security, unemployment, income distribution,[1] and the level of decision-making assigned to autonomous machines, such as cars and robots. Social media sites like Facebook, Snapchat, and Instagram share information about us, yet we do not fully understand the long-term impact this will have on our personal lives. Scientists have discovered through brain research that 5–10% of people are addicted to social media in the same way others are addicted to alcohol and drugs.[2]

The ways we conduct business have changed dramatically over the past number of years too. Webmail, chat rooms, computer technology, privacy laws and security issues have complicated the workplace. Today's leaders spent far more time in meetings than they do interacting with staff and leading their teams. While we may appear to be more connected, we are somehow further apart from one another.

Additionally, workplace and family demands have grown as we try to do more with less time. The belief was that technology would make our lives simpler and easier; yet the truth is that it has added more complexity and time to our daily lives. Multitasking has become the norm. For

---

[1] World Economic Forum, Top 9 ethical issues in artificial intelligence, Julia Bossmann, Oct 21, 2016 https://www.weforum.org/agenda/2016/10/top-10-ethical-issues-in-artificial-intelligence/

[2] The American Genius, How does social media impact your brain and body, Jennifer Walpole, September 29, 2014 https://theamericangenius.com/social-media/social-media-impact-brain-body/

example, many employees are required to carry a company phone with them to check their work voicemail and email. It is not uncommon for people to be carrying two phones: one for work and one for personal use, so they remain connected at all times both professionally and personally.

Meanwhile, family life has become more complicated. Our children are enrolled in multiple activities that can involve transporting them across cities, countries and globally. Parents are challenged to manage careers and family commitments, often leading them in different directions, complicating their ability to remain connected as a couple and family.

In the Western world, stress-related illnesses have increased, resulting in greater numbers of people with anxiety, depression and overall fatigue. The tension of managing our personal and professional lives has negatively impacted our mental wellbeing. Employees' performance issues related to anxiety and fatigue have increased. Company health-benefit providers are seeing an increase in the number of employees with mental health related illnesses as employees' try to deal with workplace stress.[3]

With the use of mobile devices and social networking sites, people are interacting less in-person while simultaneously feeling a sense of isolation and loneliness. It seems we would rather send a quick text to a friend than pick up the phone and call them or actually pay them a visit.

---

[3] Sharp Increase in Workplace Mental Health Issues, HR Director, Mark Witte, February 12, 2018 https://www.thehrdirector.com/business-news/mental-health/sharp-workplace-mental-health-issues/

The youth of today have also become addicted to mobile devices and social-networking sites rather than interacting face-to-face. Bullying has grown to include social networks, the internet and texting, negatively impacting our children and youth and leading to increased stress-related mental and physiological health issues.

Our youth are increasingly using opioids and other hallucinogens to escape the crushing pressures of modern life.[4] The global realities of the environment, war and politics have added to our level of worry, concern and sense of hopelessness. The challenges of addressing global warming, conflict and starvation seem overwhelming, and many feel helpless in making a difference.

Universally, we all want to live lives that are filled with love, happiness, fulfillment and peace. Yet our current approach to life seems to be taking us further away from those things we truly want. We say we want a slower pace of life yet continually add to our plates. We constantly buy into the marketing that insists we need more in order to

---

[4] The numbers for apparent opioid-related fatalities show a Canadian national death rate of 10.9 for every 100,000 people in the population in 2017, up from 8.2 in 2016 - The Canadian Press · Posted: Jun 19, 2018

Two-thirds of last year's drug deaths in the U.S. — about 42,000 — involved opioids, a category that includes heroin, methadone, prescription pain pills like OxyContin, and fentanyl. - The Associated Press · Posted: Dec 21, 2017

live a joyous life. As Shantideva,[5] an eighth-century Indian Buddhist monk said, "Those desiring to escape from suffering hasten right toward suffering. With the very desire for happiness, out of delusion they destroy their own happiness as if it were an enemy."

The joy we so earnestly seek cannot be found through external gratification. Only by looking within ourselves are we able to find true happiness, contentment and peace. Our joy is within us always, ever present and available when we stop to notice. By turning inwards, we are more likely to feel a sense of centredness in our being and be less affected by the natural ups and downs of life. We experience a greater sense of inner harmony and ease growing from within. Through the process of discovering inner peace, we begin to experience the external world through our lens of peace.

To create a life that is truly rewarding, we need to go through this process of discovering inner peace. We need to turn inwards to clarify what is truly important to us rather than seeking fulfillment from outside of ourselves. Getting clear about our core values enables us to choose the direction for our career, family and personal lives that will be the most satisfying. Otherwise, the opportunities to explore new and wonderful paths can cloud our vision of what is truly important at the core of our being. For many of us, life has a way of muddying the clear waters of our consciousness.

---

[5] Encyclopedia of Buddhism, Shantideva was an 8th-century Indian monk and scholar at the monastic university of Nalanda. He is best known as the author of the Bodhicaryavatara (The Way of the Bodhisattva), a classic guide to the Mahayana path that presents progressive stages to the development of compassion and wisdom (bodhicitta). https://encyclopediaofbuddhism.org/wiki/Bodhisattvacaryavatara

Pausing to reconnect to the values that are most important to us and then aligning our actions with our core values enables us to make conscious choices that give clarity of direction.

Identifying our top five values, and making choices based on those values, changes the way we engage in our personal, professional and family life. For example, if you know that spending time with family and friends is a top value, you can choose to work less and spend more time with loved ones. In this case, perhaps your career currently holds less importance for you than your family. Clarity of what we actually value provides great strength and freedom of choice and will bring more fulfillment in our lives. I have provided you a resource at the end of this book that will help you identify your own top values (see Appendix A).

Turning inward also enables us to see more clearly because it centers us in our being. Being centered allows us to feel confidence and contentment within. We know what is right for us in every moment. No longer aimlessly blowing in the wind like a leaf, we are not swayed by the plethora of options that life presents.

Knowing our true center requires the quiet observation of the experiences in life that enrich our lives as well as drain our energy. Once we determine which is which, we must have the courage to follow those things that enrich us and eliminate those things that deplete us. In doing so, we feel a greater sense of harmony, fulfilment and wellbeing growing within. We become more relaxed and at ease, as we are less influenced by extraneous and unnecessary situations. The winds of change have less influence over us. Finding inner peace is the anchor that holds us steady in turbulent waters.

Recognizing that true happiness can only be found within frees us from the illusion that happiness comes from external sources. Knowing that our thoughts and feelings are all generated from within our own mind shows us that we create our own happiness or suffering through the thoughts we nurture. We may be stirred by the external environment, but we soon realize the thoughts we have about external stimuli are our own.

Seeking happiness through external pleasure, either with things or people, can only lead to intermittent moments of delight that fade, leaving us wanting more. Consider for a moment something you wanted and thought would bring you much happiness only to find the joy was short lived and left you feeling empty. That position at work you wanted, the new car, the bigger home or that rich chocolate dessert are all external. The joy we experience in these things eventually disappears, and we are left looking for the next thing. True and lasting happiness is a state of being that resides within each of us. It is not an external thing to acquire. Being centered in ourselves, knowing what our core values are and acting on these insights fosters inner peace. Our inner happiness and joy grow the more that we align and act in accordance with our inner truth.

Practical application

To apply what you have learned in this section, try one or two of the suggestions below. Take a step, test the water or jump in with both feet. The choice is yours.

Take a step:

- Spend more time in nature. Doctors in Scotland are now prescribing time in nature to alleviate blood pressure and anxiety concerns, while increasing happiness.[6]
- Do one thing every week that makes you happy.

Test the water:

- Complete the values exercise located in Appendix A. Align your decision making with your top values moving forward.
- Purposefully spend more time interacting with family and friends.

Jump in with both feet:

- Check your email only three times a day (morning, noon and early evening).
- Turn off your work cell phone when not at work.

---

[6] BigThink, Doctors in Scotland can now prescribe nature to their patients, Evan Fleischer, Oct 12, 2018 https://bigthink.com/personal-growth/doctors-in-shetland-can-now-prescribe-a-walk-in-nature

Living in greater harmony

> *We suffer because we come in contact with*
> *so many things that are not in harmony with*
> *our real nature.*
> *~ Paramananda*

Suffering, anger and frustration are outcomes of living a life in which we are not at peace within ourselves. When we are in alignment with our true nature, our inner harmony and contentment expands. We see with greater clarity the direction we need to follow, and we are more focused in our actions. With inner contentment and clarity of direction, we are more accepting of ourselves and in turn are more accepting of others. Compassion for ourselves grows and our level of compassion for others increases as a result. By living a more harmonious life, we have greater happiness and joy in our lives.

From the moment we are born, we are on a journey of self-discovery. Not only are we learning about the world and all its wonder, but more importantly we are learning about ourselves. We are unearthing what makes us act and why. Each new day we discover something that we did not know about ourselves. There are many situations that are obvious to us, such as learning we like ice cream, action movies, or a new sport. Yet, when we look more closely at our underlying thoughts, feelings and beliefs we begin to uncover insights about ourselves that are often surprising. For example, you may learn the job you thought you always wanted is not as rewarding as you expected, the relationship you have been in for the past five years is no longer making you feel happy and passionate, or the direction your life has taken is leaving you feeling unrewarded and unfulfilled. Often in these moments, we believe it is external factors or people that are causing us to feel the way we feel.

The truth is that it is our own thoughts, feelings, and beliefs that we hold to be true that are causing us to suffer. Contemplating the areas of discord in our lives allows us to explore and realize our unconsciously held beliefs. In these moments of breakthrough, we begin to recognize that it is our held beliefs that create disharmony in our lives. Having this new awareness, we are able to make conscious choices that increase rather than decrease our sense of inner peace.

Living in a state of inner peace and harmony enables us to be clear about the direction our life needs to take and to focus on those things that increase inner peace. Coming from a place of centredness in our being, we intuitively know what the right direction for us is in any moment. When we are grounded in inner contentment, we are less swayed by the distractions of life and less likely to be influenced by those in positions of power, peers or family. Our ability to unambiguously say yes or no to people and situations becomes founded in what is true and right for us. We can choose to say no to a new job offer that does not align with our core values. We recognize that acquiring that bigger house may not provide us with a sense of financial stability. Being in a state of contentment hones our focus on those things that increase our sense of inner peace. There is great joy present in a state of contentment and we increasingly begin to choose those things and people that increase our happiness.

To live a more harmonious life, we must increasingly learn to accept all aspects of our selves. For many people, it seems odd to focus on loving ourselves. Yet, we unconsciously harbour so many negative thoughts about ourselves. It seems easy to feel love for ourselves when we are being praised or have achieved a challenging goal. We feel good about ourselves and may even experience pride and a sense of satisfaction. However, loving ourselves when we make mistakes, hurt someone's feelings or fail at something is often met with self-scorn and negation. When we see our shadow side, it may be hard to acknowledge it and face it. Perhaps you are angry at yourself for not working hard enough. Maybe you see within yourself prejudice and hatred. Perhaps you are embarrassed and ashamed to have been fired from your job. It is challenging in these moments to feel self-love. Nonetheless, loving ourselves in each and every moment, regardless of our perceived flaws, makes it possible for us to feel contentment and to be at a place of inner peace. Through our self-acceptance, we have greater capacity to be loving toward others. We recognize within the other person our own perceived imperfections, which we have already learned to appreciate and welcome. As a result of learning to live in harmony within ourselves, we become present to living in harmony with others.

Practical application

To apply what you have learned in this section, try one or two of the suggestions below. Take a step, test the water or jump in with both feet. The choice is yours.

Take a step:

- Make a list of all the things you are happy about in your life.

- Notice when you feel compelled to do something you would rather not do. Before taking action, think about what it would be like to not do it and to do it. Choose the path that aligns to your true values.

Test the water:

- Each morning, look at yourself in the mirror and say "I love you" with conviction and compassion.

- Every day, write down what you learned about yourself.

Jump in with both feet:

- Consciously choose to say no to something or someone in order to live a more peaceful life. Reflect upon the impact to both yourself and the situation or person.

- Create a vision board of what you want your life to be like in five or ten years.

Being open and receptive

> *Peace is accepting today,*
> *releasing yesterday,*
> *and giving up the need to control tomorrow.*
> *~ Lori Deschene*

When we experience a more consistent state of inner peace, we are less resistant to change and increasingly able to flow with whatever is happening in life. Our ability to remain open-minded and curious about life grows. We are more receptive to whatever life presents and more likely to meet change with wonder and enthusiasm. We are less judgemental of ourselves and in turn are less judgemental of others. There is an acceptance of life and ourselves, which we graciously extend to others. We are ever more present to being in the flow of life and less impacted by the constant change to everyday existence.

Being in the flow of life and being resilient to life's ever-changing dynamics is easier from a state of inner peace. Our day-to-day life is a reflection of the inner harmony we experience moment to moment. It takes less effort to move forward when we are flowing with the river current than swimming against it. When we are living in a harmonious state, we are accepting of where life takes us and are less concerned about controlling its direction. We are not concerned with the eddies, turns or rocks in the river because we keep returning to a place of inner contentment. And because contentment comes from within, we are not looking to find fulfillment from external sources. We have a sense of inner contentment that ebbs and flows with life's changes. This does not mean we are so detached that we are not empathetic and compassionate. It is simply that our inner peace is less impacted by the fluctuations of life. Living with an awareness of inner peace, we are conscious of these changes and accepting of what is.

In a state of contentment and harmony, our willingness to be open and receptive to new perspectives increases. When we are not living in harmony within ourselves, it is difficult for us to be interested in exploring new possibilities. Often, we are just coping with the day-to-day demands of our lives. When our jobs are not rewarding and fulfilling it is hard to take on new responsibilities. When we are struggling with our family life, we may have difficulty coping with added stress. Feeling that we are not living our life purpose, it may be hard to continue doing what we have been doing in the past. By aligning with our true nature, we drop the struggle, creating space to allow new and different opportunities to present themselves. Living in a more consistent state of inner peace, true creativity can flow from our quieted mind. Our focus is more on the joy of inner peace and less about managing life. There is a natural flow and we are in it.

We are less judgemental of ourselves and others when we are living a more harmonious life. Our self-judgements carry less weight and, in many cases, fade away. We are more accepting of our funny laugh, our perceived imperfections and our unique appearance. It is not that we are begrudgingly surrendering to things being the way they are, but rather we are simply noticing our unique characteristics without judgement. Somehow, in learning to be more at peace within ourselves, we learn to judge less and accept more. In this way, we also become more accepting of others and their choices in life.

When we are inwardly content, we have no agendas with other people. We are not looking to get something from someone or to get others to do things. We have an inner peace that is not reliant on others' actions. This does not mean our compassion for others diminishes, far from it. Inner peace is a doorway to greater openness toward ourselves and greater acceptance of others.

Practical application

To apply what you have learned in this section, try one or two of the suggestions below. Take a step, test the water or jump in with both feet. The choice is yours.

Take a step:

- Notice when you are able to flow with life and when you are resistant to it. What are you aware of about yourself?
- Notice when you are judging yourself or others. What is the perspective you are holding to be true?

Test the water:

- If you could change one thing in your life what would it be? Reflect upon what is holding you back. Take one step towards making that change.
- Where do you feel out of alignment with your true nature? Take one step to get back into alignment?

Jump in with both feet:

- In what situations do you feel content and at peace? Make a conscious choice to do those things that bring you greater peace.
- What judgements do you have about yourself? Share them with someone you trust and be open to their feedback.

Our impact

> *It is by practicing vulnerability*
> *of the heart that we discover courage.*
> ~ Chogyam Trungpa Rinpoche

Living a life based on inner peace has a positive influence on the world around us. The presence we bring, the way in which we model ourselves in the world and the language we use can have an inspiring effect on others. Whether we are aware of it or not, our presence has impact, both positive and negative. Our families, friends and colleagues all benefit from us living a life that is filled with inner harmony and contentment, as we are able to be more present for others. Finding our inner peace frees us up to bring our true selves out for the benefit of others.

Just like the ripples created by dropping a pebble into a pond, living with greater inner peace has a ripple effect that impacts others. Consider for a moment the effect you have had on other people. Think of times when, just by being who you are, you influenced others in a way that was positive. Perhaps your kindness towards a stranger was welcomed with gratitude and joy. Reflect on times when your intended impact had unintended consequences. Maybe you consciously used humour to defuse a stressful situation, but you unintentionally made things worse. Perhaps you have experienced times when someone has walked into a room and the whole atmosphere has changed, either positively or negatively. For many in the workplace, this usually happens when someone joins a meeting. Without a word being spoken, we know the energy in the room has shifted. The person's energy either infuses the meeting with positivity or shifts the discussion toward conflict or frustration. The effect one person can have can be immeasurable, but so very often we are unaware of our own impact. When we are at peace within ourselves, we bring the presence of peace to conversations, situations and events, creating greater harmony and contentment for ourselves and those around us.

The opportunity to have a positive impact on our families, friends and colleagues is substantial. When we are living with greater inner peace, waves of contentment ripple out to the people and situations around us. There is greater calm and tranquility in our homes and within our families. There is more acceptance, less judgement and an openness that allows our spouse, partners, children and extended family members to be more loving, compassionate and kind. We attract friends who are more in alignment with our own peaceful energies. Friends may seek us out just to talk and spend time with us as a result of our inner contentment. In the workplace, our inner harmony can create a calming and accepting place for people. Colleagues may ask you for advice and guidance, seeing you as grounded and calming. During meetings, you may bring a sense of composure and serenity by being more content within yourself. Being open and receptive allows for the free flow of ideas and thoughts that may not take place in a room that is less welcoming. Each of us has a profound impact on those around us simply by living a life that is more harmonious and peaceful.

Practical application

To apply what you have learned in this section, try one or two of the suggestions below. Take a step, test the water or jump in with both feet. The choice is yours.

Take a step:

- Notice the impact you have on others at work, at home or with friends. Are you having your desired impact? Consider what changes you might want to make.

- Think of someone you love to be around. What is it that you love about yourself when you are with them?

Test the water:

- Ask a trusted friend what your impact is on them. Consider if this is your desired impact and what changes you may want to consider moving forward.

- Notice how your words and tone of voice impact other people around you. Play with a more peaceful tone of voice and notice your impact.

Jump in with both feet:

- Ask your family or a work colleague what your impact is on them, including what they want more or less of and what changes they suggest you make to have your desired impact on others?

Chapter Two: The dance of dynamic peace

*Peace is not the absence of conflict;
but the ability to cope with it.
~ Mahatma Gandhi*

What is inner peace?

Peace.
It does not mean to be in a place where there is no noise,
trouble or hard work. It means to be in
the midst of all those things
and still be calm in your heart.
~ Unknown

Typically, when we think about peace, we envision a world in which there is no war, conflict or struggle, where we live amongst each other in a state of harmony and acceptance. Some may feel this is an unrealistic, utopian state that is not possible to either experience or create. It is easy to understand this view when we look at the outer world. It is clear we have little to no control over what happens in the world. However, if we begin within ourselves, we soon recognize we do have control over our thoughts and how we view our world.

Through an ongoing exploration of self-discovery and acceptance, we are able to experience ever increasing states of calm and contentment. We have less of an inner desire to be other than who we are, and we increasingly find ourselves in a state of greater inner serenity. This does not imply that we will not experience the ups and downs of life. Rather, our foundation in peace becomes solid in the acceptance of ourselves as we are, having taken the time to go inward, to know what is important to us and to align our actions with our core values.

Over two thousand years ago, an inscription on an interior wall of the Temple of Apollo at Delphi stated, "know thyself." Our ancestors knew that we must, above all else, know ourselves, and this truth continues to be relevant even today. We cannot change the outer world without first looking inward and changing our inner viewpoint.

Our perception of reality is based on the inner lens from which we view it. This lens we use to view our world determines whether we view things as good or bad, positive or negative, or indifferent. It affects our emotions and mood. If we change the lens through which we view the world our perspective changes. For example, the disappointment you feel about not getting the promotion you want can be changed when you consider the myriad of possibilities that are now available.

Our perception may also be limited by our ability to see things for what they are. Consider our physical body. It appears solid to us, and yet at the molecular level, there is a great deal of space between the smallest of molecules. Our perception and belief are that we are solid because that is what we see. And yet we are in fact spacious.

Similarly, the beliefs that we hold to be true about the world we experience are filtered through the lens of our beliefs. If we are experiencing life as challenging and a struggle, we must begin to look at the beliefs and thoughts that are running through our mind. Consider a time in your life when you were struggling with a decision or a situation. A key part of the inner conflict was the belief that you held that the situation was difficult. If you were able to change your belief, the effort to resolve the situation would have lessened.

When inner conflict arises, pausing to take the time to reflect and contemplate what is really going on underneath enables us to see long-held perspectives that are not serving us in the moment. Dropping such beliefs is not easy, yet through awareness and the ongoing self-reflection of our inner challenges, we begin to erode the hold that our beliefs have over us. We see that at some point they served a purpose in our lives but that now they are no longer helping us live a life of contentment. Seeing our challenges and inner conflicts with awareness and self-acceptance begins to change the lens through which we view the world. For example, many of us we hold the belief that we are not worthy of love. We hide our belief behind the mask of being a people pleaser. Yet, when let go of this belief and learn to love and accept ourselves we also let go of the need to please others. By learning the way our beliefs influence our experience of life, we increasingly learn to be more at peace with people and situations and less at odds within ourselves.

What is this experience of greater inner peace? Profound stillness fills the body at the same time as we relinquish our external focus. Conscious awareness is both present and aware of itself. We feel a sense of centredness in who we are and are more accepting of life as it. We have moments with no inner conflict or struggle. We are tranquil within ourselves, and we are able to be fully present in each moment.

Reflect on moments in your life when you felt a sense of inner peace and contentment. Perhaps it was at the moment of a perfect sunset or sunrise. Maybe it was the peaceful solitary moment of stillness you experienced sitting in nature, overlooking a vast valley of lush green forest. Possibly it was the moment your child or grandchild was born. Each of us has experienced such moments of stillness and calm where we felt a sense of inner peace. It is in these moments that it seems as though the world pauses, and we became present in the here and now.

As we look deeper into the layers of our consciousness and unconsciousness, we eventually begin to experience more and more moments of inner contentment. Each new discovery is like watching a lotus opening its petals, revealing its full beauty for all to see. Indeed, the more we are able and willing to look at our blemishes and scars with self-acceptance, the more we are able to feel at peace with ourselves. Knowing ourselves and acting in alignment with what is truly important to us at the core of our being enables us to blossom into our own lotus flower. Out of the mud of conflicting beliefs and thoughts, we are able to embrace our beauty with truthful awareness and acceptance.

From this foundation of inner contentment and peace, we are able to better weather the storms of everyday life. Undoubtedly, life is full of ups and downs. Surprises occur regularly. Life rarely unfolds how we expect it to. Yet, when we are continuously learning about ourselves and courageously exploring everything that surfaces, we develop the ability to be with life's volatility in ways that are accepting. We see more clearly that life is not static but rather dynamic. Our inner peace moves with whatever life has in store for us and we are able to be in the flow of life because we are open to and accepting of what is happening.

Consider a time when you were resistant to change and think about the level of stress and discomfort that it created for you. Would your experience have been different if you were able to embrace whatever was happening rather than resist it? All too often, our resistance to life originates within our thoughts, feelings and beliefs about how it should be instead of how it is. We are so easily locked into our own tunnel vision of life rather than being open to new possibilities. There is both great humility and liberation in the experiential knowing that we are simply travellers witnessing life unfolding, and that there is truly nothing we have control over, not even our own breath.

Only through this journey of self-awareness, discovery and acceptance can we truly be at a place of inner peace. Our willingness to look inward and explore with curiosity whatever is arising in our consciousness determines our ability to move through our limiting perspectives about life and ourselves. We courageously face whatever truth surfaces, regardless of how uncomfortable the reality. Through wakeful self-observation and reflection, the layers of our humanness reveal themselves, and we are freed like a butterfly emerging from its cocoon.

Moments of transformation can be both uncomfortable and painless. From our own life, we know that some of life's lessons seem easier to assimilate than others. Yet, we need not feel both the pain of transformation and suffering simultaneously. As the butterfly transforms, it must experience some physical pain in the metamorphosis from a caterpillar to a butterfly. But it need not suffer with the lack of acceptance of its transformation. Can it choose not to transform? We too are continuously transforming. Change is constant and we can accept it with openness, curiosity and eagerness or resist it and experience increasing amounts of inner suffering. Seeing our limiting beliefs with awareness, we learn to let them go like a caterpillar shedding its outer skin. We only suffer when we hold onto limiting beliefs. When we willingly release held perspectives that no longer serve us, we are liberated.

The dance

> *Nothing troubles me.*
> *I offer no resistance to trouble;*
> *therefore, it does not stay with me.*
> *~ Sri Nisargadatta Maharaj*

The dance of dynamic peace is a continuous journey of self-discovery and exploration. There is no final end-state that we achieve, but rather the endless revealing of layers of deeper consciousness. The idea of a utopian state of inner peace suggests a final destiny in which there is an end to the unfolding of life. Yet, conscious awareness cannot be created or destroyed because it is the ever-present eternal witness to what is. It is the natural life force that is eternally present within everything and everyone. At the core of our being, our true nature is inner peace and it is available whenever we are present enough to be in the experience of it. Yet, in our day-to-day lives, we move between the grace of letting things unfold and the drive of purposeful action. Ultimately, whether we are allowing things to unfold or driving toward a goal, all paths lead to the same outcome in our journey: the discovery of ever-increasing inner peace.

We are forever expanding and contracting in our consciousness as life unfolds moment to moment. With every new experience, we learn something new about ourselves that we then integrate into conscious awareness. Therefore, life is like a dance with movement, turns, swooshes, and dips from which we discover different aspects of ourselves. Each moment is unlike the last, as we are never the same from one moment to the next. Even the cells within our body are constantly dying and rejuvenating. From an evolutionary perspective, the changes are often subtle, and we do not notice them day to day. Over time though, our face ages, our hair changes colour and perhaps we move a bit slower. We grow from an embryo into a child, into an adult and into a senior before the body typically dies. Throughout this physical transformation, our conscious awareness is also transformed as we integrate all of our thoughts, feelings and experiences. Occasionally, there is revolutionary change, usually after we experience a life-altering experience, such as the loss of a loved one, the ravages of war and tyranny or the impact of a natural disaster.

During our lifetime, we integrate, to a lesser or greater degree, our life experiences into our consciousness, thus shaping and transforming us into the person we are in this very moment. Even at the death of our physical body, our consciousness continues onto more subtle levels of awareness. Einstein said, "Energy cannot be created or destroyed, it can only be changed from one form to another."[7] So too is our energy constantly being transformed physically, mentally, emotionally and consciously. We are dynamic beings, forever transforming in this dance of the expansion and contraction of conscious awareness.

Inner peace continues to transform us as we experience our dynamic lives filled with the myriad and varied journeys of life. We cannot therefore view inner peace as a static achieved state. Rather, it is a state of being that changes and evolves with life. As our conscious awareness grows and we integrate new experiences, our inner peace shifts and changes as well. What was once challenging and difficult to face is now a momentary observation that passes like a cloud in a blue sky. We are transformed as we face our

---

[7] AZ Quotes; https://www.azquotes.com/author/4399-Albert_Einstein/tag/energy

fears, such as the fear of public speaking, living on our own or jumping off a high diving board. Eventually, our inner peace is less disturbed by external factors and becomes a more constant state of being. As our lives transform before our eyes there remains the calm, wakeful observer that is at the core of our inner peace. This observer is our conscious awareness, the ever-present witness to the unfolding of life in each and every moment.

Our true nature is one of inner peace. It is ever-present, alert and awake in the observation of what is happening. A calm presence has learned to dance with the wind while remaining at peace within itself. There is a grace in allowing whatever is unfolding to be revealed with acceptance and non-judgement. At the core of our being there is an inner wise sage who knows that life unfolds as it should and that we are merely observers. With this awareness, there is no rush to achieve, to accomplish or to obtain. All that is needed or wanted is provided in the present moment. Yet, we hear the voice in our heads calling us to walk down another path or climb another hill. Our sense of inner peace shows us that if we move forward in action that is aligned with our core values, we are able to do so in a way that fosters greater inner contentment. We feel greater joy when we accept a job that excites us and utilizes our skills. When we carve out time for those things that are most important to us (e.g., family, travel, exercise) we feel happier and more content. If we stay on the path that calls to our being, we intuitively know it will lead to more joy and bliss. Each person's path is unique to them and will have its own turns and crossroads to be journeyed, yet the dance between allowing life to happen and taking purposeful action still determines the degree to which we experience inner peace.

Experiential knowing

> *It is the contemplative man*
> *who is full of joy and peace.*
> ~ Paramananda

To know inner peace, we must experientially know contentment and stillness. It cannot be conceptually realized. The degree to which we are willing to look deeply into our consciousness and unconsciousness, with eyes wide open, determines the degree to which we can experience inner peace. Courageously being willing to explore whatever thoughts, feelings, emotions and beliefs that surface enables us to live on a strong foundation of inner harmony. Finding our own answers by curiously looking at whatever surfaces allows us to make conscious decisions that are congruent with our soul's purpose. Experientially knowing what is at the core of our being allows us to reside in a pool of contentment and peace. Living in a state of greater inner harmony, not only benefits us, but is of benefit to all beings. Knowing ourselves better and living a content life, we become like a flame drawing in the moth so that others can experience the contentment of a peaceful life too.

We can only obtain knowledge of inner harmony through an experiential event. In the observation of a still and present moment, the flowering of inner peace occurs. Our attention becomes focused on the immediate moment. A sense of calm and tranquility rises up in our being, and we relax into the here and now. The mind quiets, and the space between our thoughts widens. Our consciousness expands, and we feel serene bliss embracing us. Judgement and evaluation are suspended and surrendered gleefully. Pause for a few minutes and take three slow deep breaths.

Listen to the sound of your inhalation and exhalation. Notice the increased euphoria rising within your body. Feel a sense of calm and tranquility surfacing like a well of spring water rising out of the ground. Become aware of the sensation of inner peace materializing in your awareness. Inner peace is ever present and available whenever we take the time to be still and notice.

Periods of inner peace increase our willingness to face our fears and challenges with open curiosity. The artificial walls we have created in our mind begin to fall, and we are able to move forward in ways we never imagined possible. Courageously facing our fears can be challenging and scary. In many cases, even though our walls may be self-imposed, they can feel like towers and barriers too difficult to scale or cross. Our thoughts, feelings and beliefs are deeply engrained in our consciousness and can be tough to overcome. Being aware of the stories and perspectives we have running behind the scenes in our consciousness allows us to see and acknowledge that there is a barrier.

In some instances, when we immediately recognize an inner narrative is false, we can easily discard the story that is running in our head. However, some long-held beliefs may be both difficult to see and difficult to let go of. It was Shakespeare, in "Julius Caesar," who wrote, "The eye sees not itself but by reflection, by some other things."[8] We cannot see ourselves unless we look in a mirror or other reflective surface and see the person who is looking. The people, situations and events that come in to our lives are our mirrors. It may be difficult for us to see our held beliefs

---

[8] Julius Caesar, William Shakespeare, 1599

and storylines because we are so often right in the middle of them. Yet, it may be more obvious to others, who are not running the same story in their heads. At times, we may not be ready or willing to drop the storyline, as our egos are caught up in upholding our beliefs as true. In these instances, it may be helpful to seek help from professionals, such as a personal coach, counsellor or spiritual teacher, to help you explore the issue from a detached observation.

The more we are able to step back and look at our thoughts and feelings from a meta view, the easier we can truly see the implications and limitations of our long-held beliefs. Some held beliefs may not change immediately and may take time to overcome. Beliefs build up over time and can take considerable time to dismantle. For example, deeply rooted beliefs of low personal value, worth and esteem may take years to overcome. In these moments, it is essential to be patient, loving and compassionate with ourselves. We are not broken or wrong, we are simply holding a perspective that may no longer be of benefit to us.

The answers to our questions are always within us, we just need to be willing to look with curiosity and be open to new possibilities. From a place of inner peace, there is spacious room for acceptance and exploration of whatever is surfacing in our consciousness. Our walls are down and we are able to consider alternate perspectives from the view that we have of our inner and external worlds. In seeing our storyline, we can pause and see that it is in fact a narrative that we have created within ourselves. Fearlessly, with all thoughts, feelings and beliefs, we need to ask ourselves, "Is this true?" Is it true I will be a failure if I don't get that new job? Is it true I am unworthy of love and companionship? Is it true I have to be perfect for others to accept me? In these moments, we are conscious awareness looking back on ourselves to see the reality of our own creations and to challenge ourselves to see what is truthful and what is illusory. Reflecting on our inner response, in a space of acceptance and non-judgement, allows us to discover for ourselves the true nature of reality and to let go of fictitious perspectives. Only within this experiential knowing are we able to drop long-held beliefs. We come to know the truth provided by our inner voice, as it is profound in its clarity and honesty. This journey to inner peace begins on the meditator's seat.

Practical application

To apply what you have learned in this section, try one or two of the suggestions below. Take a step, test the water or jump in with both feet. The choice is yours.

Take a step:

- Begin to observe life as dynamic and ever changing.
- Reflect on your experience of inner peace. What are you aware of?

Test the water:

- Sit comfortably. Observe how you feel mentally and emotionally. Take three slow deep breaths. Now notice how you feel after pausing to breathe.
- Notice how others react around you when you are stressed and when you are peaceful.

Jump in with both feet:

- Where do you feel frustrated in your life? Look at the underlying belief that is the basis for this frustration. Challenge yourself by asking, "Is this belief true?" Then, looking at what expectation is not being met and take action to resolve your frustration based upon your observations.

- What fear(s) hold you back from embracing life fully? Choose one fear and take action to face it and overcome it.

Chapter Three: Meditation

*If you know how to let go and be at peace,
you know everything you need to know
about living in the world.*
~ Ajahn Brahm

What is meditation?

> *The purpose of meditation is
> personal transformation.*
> ~ Henepola Gunaratana

One of the best teachings I received on meditation was offered by my first meditation teacher, Master Charles Cannon. He taught that "meditation is the observation of what is."[9] At first glance, this teaching seems to be a simple and straightforward description, yet it holds so much more truth and experiential understanding of the meditator's journey.

Meditation is founded on our ability to be fully present with whatever surfaces in the mind with awareness, non-judgement and detached observation. As a result of this developed skill, meditators experience a deceleration in brainwave frequencies that allows for a stronger synchronization of the mind and body.[10]

Many people say they are unable to meditate because their minds are too busy. Yet, this is precisely the reason one should sit to meditate. In the journey of self-discovery, meditation is one of the best practices to finding inner peace and contentment.

Meditation is the developed ability to observe our thoughts, feelings and beliefs without attachment or

---

[9] Master Charles, Synchronicity Foundation Inc., Virginia, USA
[10] Health and Human Services, Redirecting Brain Waves: Examining the Effects of Meditation on the Brain, Rebecca Bernstein, August 25, 2016 https://www.tuw.edu/health/effects-of-meditation-on-the-brain/

judgement. When we meditate, we gaze inwardly, witnessing surfacing thoughts and emotions. A typical analogy that is used by meditation teachers to describe this experience is that of watching clouds passing in the sky. We see our thoughts surface and pass without trying to jump onto them. Another analogy used by Master Charles Cannon is that of watching a parade. The only way to see a whole parade is as an observer watching the floats as they go by. The moment we jump onto a float, our perspective of the parade becomes limited to our view from that float. Thus, our surfacing thoughts are like a parade's floats passing by in our mind.

The intention of meditation is not to stop the mind from thinking but rather to be in the observation of the mind. The greater our effort to stop the mind from thinking, the more it seems the mind thinks. It is like trying to put a lid on a pot of boiling water. Eventually, the water will boil over. Alternatively, when we are not holding onto our thoughts they easily pass, creating space for the next thought to surface. Our mind is designed to think; that is its job. It is important to remember that when we try to alter our mind's true nature, we only create greater agitation and stress for ourselves.

As we practice meditation, the space between thoughts grows with moments of deep stillness. During these periods of stillness, we remain present in the observation of whatever surfaces but without attachment. The moment we become attached to a thought or to stillness, it is like we have just jumped onto the float.

So, what do non-attachment and non-judgement mean in the context of the practice of meditation? Non-attachment is our ability to remain an observer to the parade of thoughts and feelings that surface when we meditate instead of jumping onto a passing float. When we attach ourselves to surfacing thoughts, we have become identified with it. For example, you have a disagreement with a work colleague, and you cannot stop thinking about it. Your thoughts become so intertwined in it that you are not able to separate yourself and see it just as an event. In this case, you have become attached to your thoughts about the situation. A non-attached perspective would be that a situation occurs at work and you are aware of it, but you do not become caught up in the situation. You are able to remain the detached witness to the event. Typically, with attachment, we have an expectation about how something should be or how we want it to be. Our belief about the situation is so strong that we cannot see other points of view. When we cling onto thoughts, we create stress within ourselves that disrupts our inner peace. From a meditator's perspective, we are able to see the thoughts surface in our consciousness and simply let them pass.

Non-judgement is our ability to see our thoughts surface and not evaluate them as good or bad, positive or negative. They are just thoughts. During meditation, we often judge ourselves when thoughts surface. As an example, the judgemental thought that I won't be able to find a pair of pants I like because I am too skinny. Or perhaps we think of a recent interaction with our spouse, and we simultaneously judge ourselves for having responded abruptly to them. This is often why new meditators say, "I can't meditate" or "I've been thinking the whole time I was supposed to be meditating." But what is important is that meditation is a practice. It is not about perfecting it in our first sit. As we practice meditation, we are able to see our judgemental mind for what it is and choose to merely notice our thoughts instead. In this way, our judgements and thoughts come and go, passing like the clouds in the sky or the floats in a parade. As a meditator, our role is to practice simply seeing them for what they are and allowing them to float on by.

Our thoughts are generated by the cells in our brain, called neurons, communicating with each other using electrical impulses that make wavelike patterns, called brainwaves. Both the frequency (i.e., number of brainwaves per second) and the amplitude (number of neurons sending an electrical impulse at the same time and speed) of our brainwaves change depending on the information they are conveying.[11] When we meditate, the frequency and amplitude of our brainwave activity slows down and lengthens.[12] We can look at what this means by understanding the different types of brainwaves. Researchers have categorized brainwaves according to their frequency patterns. Beta waves have the highest frequency, followed by alpha, theta, delta and gamma waves, respectively.[13] A graphic illustration of these five types of brainwave activity can be found below (see Image 1).

In our normal everyday life, we are busy people with families, careers and commitments. We need to be thinking and responding all the time to events, situations and people.

---

[11] Australian Academy of Science, People and medicine: Just Think... Dr. Bernadette Fitzgibbon, Dr. Manreena Kaur, Dr. Kaori Ikeda, Hayley Teasdale, https://www.science.org.au/curious/people-medicine/eeg

[12] Brainwave Meditation, Brain Waves and States of Mind https://meditation-brainwave.blogspot.com/2018/11/brain-activity-and-meditation-brainwaves.html

[13] Mental Health Daily, https://mentalhealthdaily.com/2014/04/15/5-types-of-brain-waves-frequencies-gamma-beta-alpha-theta-delta/

In this state of being, our brainwaves are predominantly beta. In this range, the frequency is high (16-30 Hz) and the amplitude is very low. When we slow down, such as on a walk in the park or when listening to relaxing music, our brainwaves shift from beta to alpha. We feel less rushed and more tranquil. The brainwaves have slowed a bit (8-15 Hz) and the amplitude is low. As we settle in for a good night's sleep, our brainwaves shift from alpha to theta. Often this is described as the state just before we fall asleep. Our brainwaves become more rounded and stretched out, meaning the frequency has decreased (4–7 Hz), while the amplitude is low to medium. This is the threshold between being conscious and unconscious. The next stage is delta and that occurs when we are asleep. When delta waves are predominant, we have entered the realm of our unconsciousness, allowing our minds to process thoughts from the day. Our brainwave frequency is at its lowest levels (0.1–3 Hz) and the amplitude is high.

Gamma brainwaves were previously unknown until scientists began using digitally electroencephalography (EEG). Neuroscientists believe that gamma brainwaves have the ability to connect all areas of brain.[14] Individuals whose awareness is focused on compassion, love and altruism experience strong gamma brainwave activity.[15] When we practice meditation, we transcend through, beta, alpha, theta and delta states of consciousness. We begin to slow,

---

[14] Mind Valley, The Marvelous Properties of Gamma Brain Waves, Cheyenne Diaz, January 17, 2018 https://blog.mindvalley.com/gamma-brain-waves/
[15] BrainWorks, What are Brainwaves? https://brainworksneurotherapy.com/what-are-brainwaves

which allows us to experience the calm and serene state of being that is always present when we take the time to notice. As a result of one's meditative practice, individuals are more readily able to access these states of universal love and kindness (gamma state).

Image 1

HUMAN BRAIN WAVES

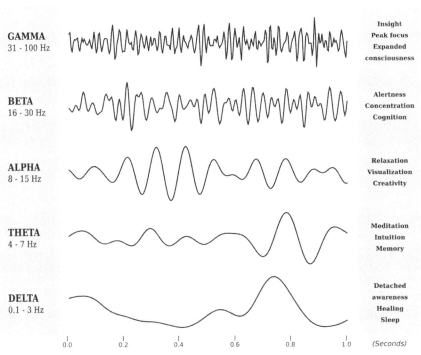

As our brainwave activity slows down during meditation, we can experience moments of mental, emotional and physical upheaval. Through our experiences in life, we store memories and energy within our bodies. Most of us can remember experiences from as early as our childhood. Some of our memories have emotions associated with them, and these emotions surface along with our memories. Recollections about a deceased relative, our first love or the birth of our children bring up emotions we have stored in our bodies. In the same way, we also store energy in our body from our past experiences. We may have nervous energy from a past disturbing experience. We may experience tension headaches or have trauma stored in our body from horrific experiences. All of these experiences have an associated energy that gets deposited into our bodies and consciousness.

When we slow down our brainwave frequency during meditation, any experience that we have stored in our bodies that is at a higher frequency of vibration than our decelerated state, must be released. This phenomenon can manifest during meditation as physical pain, fidgeting, obsessive thinking or emotional releases, such as crying or laughing. These are normal experiences during meditation, especially when you are first learning how to meditate. As your practice deepens, the regularity of these experiences will lessen, and you will more often be able to remain a detached witness.

Many people believe they are unable to meditate, saying they have tried but are incapable of quieting their mind. It is unfortunate that their early experience of meditation was based on the belief that their mind should be completely still. Meditation has never been about quieting the mind but rather being in the observation of it and ultimately transcending beyond the mind. A quiet mind is the by-product of a regular meditation practice. Ajahn Amaro, a Theravada Buddhist monk and teacher suggests, "The best way to deal with excessive thinking is to just listen to it, to listen to the mind. Listening is much more effective than trying to stop thought or cut it off."16 Here Ajahn Amaro reinforces the perspective that we simply notice our thoughts instead of trying to suppress them. Meditation presents us with the opportunity to see our thoughts with a detached observation. When we are able to remain detached, there is no incremental charge, neither attraction nor repulsion, but rather the calm witnessing of whatever comes up as a passing thought.

Practical application

To apply what you have learned in this section, try one or two of the suggestions below. Take a step, test the water or jump in with both feet. The choice is yours.

Take a step:

- Notice periods of stillness or calm either just before falling asleep or just as you wake up.
- Recognize the busy brainwave state at work and compare it to times when you are more relaxed (e.g., in nature or unwinding at home at the end of the day). What do you notice, and how can you create greater peace throughout your day?

Test the water:

- Notice what events or situations cause you to become stressed or anxious. What are the underlying thoughts and feelings about the event or situation?

---

[16] AZ Quotes, Ajahn Amaro https://www.azquotes.com/author/25171-Ajahn_Amaro

Are your thoughts or feelings true or just a belief about how it should be?

- Sit quietly for 5–10 minutes and simply watch the parade of thoughts that go by. Notice if there are some thoughts that you become attached to. What insight about yourself can you gather from these thoughts?

Jump in with both feet:

- Observe the energy in emotional situations (e.g., laughter, anger, frustration, love). See how each state has an energetic feel to it. What insight do you have about yourself?

- Think about a traumatic incident in your life. Notice the emotions, pain and/or suffering still present within the body. Meditate on the incident and see what surfaces.

Why meditate?

> *If you truly want to discover a lasting sense of peace and contentment, you need to learn to rest your mind.*
> ~Yongey Mingyur Rinpoche

Novice and seasoned meditators are often faced with the question, "Why meditate?" In the initial stages of meditation there are four obvious reasons why someone would develop a regular meditative practice. First, our minds become more still and focused as a result of meditation, thus improving our ability to concentrate while enhancing our creative ability. Second, we develop the ability to be more present with our emotions rather than being carried away by them. A regular meditative practice has positive physiological benefits for our circulatory and nervous systems. Third, meditation puts us in touch with deeper aspects of self and spirit. As we become a more seasoned meditator, the question of why we meditate turns toward the ongoing curious exploration of deeper aspects of self. Just like peeling back the layers of an onion, there are more and more subtle facets of self-discovery that lead to profound awakenings and illuminations. Fourth, we ultimately meditate to reveal to ourselves the true nature of existence. This revelation can only be experienced through a meditative practice and cannot be conveyed in words. Through the process of having a regular and prolonged meditative practice, we experience a more consistent state of peace and tranquility within our being. We are better able to witness the dance of dynamic peace.

When we first begin to practice meditation, one of the initial benefits we notice is an improved ability to focus and concentrate on tasks in our daily lives. We develop the ability to quiet our mind and be a witness to whatever is happening in our mind in each moment. A regular meditation practice, at least in the early stages, typically includes an object of focus. During meditation, we give our busy mind a job, such as to observe the breath or repeat a mantra (i.e., a word or sound repeated to aid concentration in meditation[17]). This ongoing practice of focusing on something during meditation aids in developing the skill to remain focused on one thing at a time rather than being distracted by multiple thoughts colliding all at once. Developing this skill is especially important in the twenty-first century as we are conditioned to be multitaskers. Our work life involves numerous emails, e-chats, phone calls and continuous interruptions. Through it all, we are expected to respond promptly to incoming inquiries from colleagues and/or clients while being productive and delivering results. Even our children are learning to be multitaskers from an early age. They are texting with friends while playing a video game and/or watching television. In a multitasking environment, we experience a frenzied, scattered energy as we try to handle all the stimulation coming at us. Meditation trains us to slow down, and to be focused on one thought, one task at a time. Our awareness shifts from a past or future focus to the present moment: the only true moment we have. A regular meditation practice entrains our mind and body to observe the busyness of life with a calm, wakeful watching. Ironically, as a result of this focused, calm witnessing, we are able to be more productive in our work and lives. Our ability to remain focused grows and we naturally become

---

[17] English Oxford Living Dictionary

more single-focused, enhancing our ability to experience greater states of peace and serenity.

Through a meditative practice, we develop the ability to be more present to whatever emotion is coming up for us with a detached witnessing. Emotions arising out of our thoughts can positively or negatively impact our ability to be at peace. This is especially true at times when the part of our brain called the amygdala is activated by fear to initiate a fight or flight response within the body. When fear, anxiety or worry surface, they can be all consuming and can take us away from this very moment. Perhaps you fear the loss of a loved one and you worry obsessively. Maybe you have just been told by your doctor that you have a serious health issue which brings up your fear of dying. In these moments, our bodies release hormones in response to our emotions, and we may feel helpless to manage them. But when we meditate regularly, we slowly develop the ability to see our fears and anxiety with a detached observation. We are able to perceive these strong emotions just like our thoughts, as passing clouds in our consciousness. As we also practice non-judgement, we become more patient with ourselves and better able to remain detached. We see when we are hooked by our emotions and thoughts, yet their impact on us is softened as we are better able to remain the witness to them.

This experience is also true when we have equally strong emotions of love and joy that surface. While these feelings typically do not trigger our fight or flight response, they can have equal impact in terms of their intensity. We are often drawn toward these emotions that generate perceived positive feelings. The pleasure of finding love for the first time or the joy of seeing a close family member you have not seen in a long time brings up powerful feelings of tenderness. In these moments, we experience such joyous emotions that we do not want to see them end. We believe the other person is the cause of our feelings of love and joy. Our desire to keep feeling this pleasure triggers us and we cling to the person that brings up these blissful feelings. Yet, this misplaced belief hides the truth that our feelings are our own and cannot be created by another person. The people and situations that seem to bring us joy are in fact the catalysts that help us remember and re-experience the feelings of pleasure and love that are always present and available within us. The external world is our mirror into ourselves, helping us remember our true nature, which is one of love, compassion and kindness.

Through the practice of meditation, our intent is not to supress or ignore our positive and negative emotions but rather to experience them with conscious awareness. Along our meditator's journey, we are increasingly able to be the witness to whatever emotion surfaces. We see love surface, and we are aware of it. Feelings of fear and anxiety emerge and we are able to be in the observation of them. There is no clinging to or pushing away of emotions. Our emotions, just like our thoughts, provide us with insight and perspective on how we are perceiving our world. When we can be the observer of our thoughts and feelings without judgement, we become the witness to the parade as it passes by. We are able to see from a broader point of view, expanding our limiting perspectives. Then, should we consciously choose to jump onto a float (an emotion or thought), we can do so with awareness and curiosity to see what the journey has in store for us.

There are numerous physiological benefits arising out of a regular meditation practice. As a result of meditation, we can experience an improvement in our cardiovascular system. Our blood pressure and heart rate decrease as a result of a regular meditation practice.[18] As the mind and body slow down during meditation, we feel calmer and more peaceful. There is less stress on our bodies as we let go and relax. There have also been studies that have shown a regular meditation practice can reduce and maintain body weight.[19] Through meditation we can become more aware of our stress-related eating habits, which can help in terms of managing our consumption of food.

Meditation increases our awareness of our thoughts and emotions. Through this heightened awareness, we more easily see our trigger points and can make conscious choices about which thoughts we entertain and which we can simply observe. Meditation is also beneficial for our nervous system.[20] Experiencing a more calm and peaceful state of being helps to reduce our anxiety, improve our sleep and alleviate our depression. When we are better able to be the witness to our thoughts and emotions, we are more capable of managing our anxiety levels. As we continue to

---

[18] verywell Health, Meditation for Help to Lower High Blood Pressure, Cathy Wong (Reviewed by Richard N. Fogoros, MD) September 14, 2017 https://www.verywellhealth.com/meditation-for-high-blood-pressure-can-it-help-89622

[19] WebMD, Does Mediation Help You Lose Weight, Jenn Horton, Reviewed by Elizabeth Klodas, MD, FACC on August 01, 2014 https://www.webmd.com/balance/features/meditation-hypertension-and-weight-loss#1

[20] EOC Institute, Meditation/Meditation Relaxes Your Nervous System https://eocinstitute.org/meditation/meditation-relaxes-your-nervous-system/

practice meditation, we develop the ability to be detached from our emotions and thoughts. Consequently, we are able to be more of the observer of the obsessive feelings that are creating our anxiety and we are better able to cope with the waves of emotions.[21]

A peaceful and calm mind helps us to fall asleep more easily. When we are feeling settled within ourselves, there is less stress and tension. We are able to relax and allow ourselves to fall asleep. Should we wake up and find that our minds are busy, our meditative practice supports us in watching the mind rather than being caught up in our thoughts. We are aware of our preoccupied thoughts and are able to practice a detached observation. So much of our thinking is based in the past or future. This can be especially true at night. Thoughts about the day or what tomorrow will bring keep our minds busy and impede our natural sleep cycle. Meditation helps us practice being present to this very moment. Whenever we are able to be in the current moment, our awareness expands, our breathing slows, and we feel more at peace. We are able to rest the mind and allow sleep to once again blanket us.

Having a regular meditative practice can also alleviate the challenges caused by depression. Meditation results in the release of endorphins and neurotransmitters that increase a sense of happiness and wellbeing within the body.[22] We experience a greater sense of joy and contentment

---

[21] The Chopra Center, Deepak Chopra M.D., Articles: How Meditation can Help Anxiety https://chopra.com/articles/how-meditation-can-help-anxiety

[22] The Guided Mediation Site, Mediation and Depression https://www.the-guided-meditation-site.com/meditation-and-depression.html

as a result of meditation. Being able to observe our thoughts with non-attachment and non-judgement, we are able to see the spiralling negative thought patterns as they occur. We can then choose to reshape our thoughts in a way that is positive and uplifting.

More recent research suggests that meditation has a positive impact on our immune system. Researchers have discovered that a regular meditative practice positively activates our t-cells and antibody production to fight invading foreign bodies.[23] When there is less stress in our physical body, we are better able to experience peace and contentment throughout our whole being.

A more traditional perspective of meditation identifies the benefits arising from an increase in self-awareness. Awareness is the first step in the process of seeing the world from a new vantage point. Only through awareness are we able to change. Thus, meditation is a tool we use to help us remove the blinders of our unconsciousness. Once we remove the blinders, our view of the world shifts. Perhaps you have strong feelings of hatred for someone who you believe has done you wrong. As a meditator, you are aware of the hatred that has surfaced. You are also aware of your judgement that they should have acted in a different way, which is the right way according to your held belief about how it should be. Now you can see your belief that people should act a certain way and that this person has not behaved in alignment with your held belief.

---

[23] EOC Institute, How the Mind can Boost Immunity, Multiple Health & Conquer Disease https://eocinstitute.org/meditation/boosting-your-immune-system-with-meditation/

Seeing our unconscious beliefs allows us to challenge underlying assumptions and release beliefs that cause our suffering. Other people do not cause our suffering. It is our own thoughts and beliefs that cause our suffering. We suffer because of the beliefs we cling to in order to maintain our perspective of the world. For most of us, we will continue to suffer until we let go of the beliefs that prevent us from seeing the world as it truly is. A meditative practice unpacks the layers of our limiting thoughts and releases us from our self-inflicted suffering. The experience of a meditation teacher can help to point out the eddies along the way so that we do not get entangled in our own unconsciousness.

Meditation is also not limited to any one religion or belief system. It crosses all cultures, sects and faiths. Regardless of our affiliations or beliefs, meditation helps us to get in touch with whatever we call spirit or God. When we slow down and are able to feel our heart beating, there is a sense of serene relaxation that comes over us. In moments when we are present enough to hear the sound of silence, we are filled with a profound and eternal peace and tranquility. When we feel love and compassion for another being, we are touched with an ever-expanding sense of delight. These are the moments when we are connected to spirit. This is our true state of being, which is luminous love, compassion and bliss. Words pale in comparison to the experience of being in touch with spirit. The thirteenth-century poet and mystic, Jalāl ad-Dīn Muhammad Rūmī, tries to describe the experience of love by beautifully articulating the futility of words.

> Both light and shadow
> are the dance of Love.
> Love has no cause;
> it is the astrolabe of God's secrets.
> Lover and Loving are inseparable
> and timeless.
> Although I may try to describe Love,
> when I experience it, I am speechless.
> Although I may try to write about Love
> I am rendered helpless;
> my pen breaks and the paper slips away
> at the ineffable place
> where Lover, Loving and Loved are one.
> Every moment is made glorious
> by the light of Love.

Meditation is the doorway to return home to our true selves. It pulls back the veils of our unconsciousness, revealing our true nature to ourselves. This experience can be both blissfully liberating and challenging. When we pull back the layers of our unconsciousness there may be areas of ourselves we would prefer not to see. It is only by turning toward whatever surfaces and learning to love all aspects of ourselves that we experience a deep and profound sense of inner peace and contentment.

Practical application

To apply what you have learned in this section, try one or two of the suggestions below. Take a step, test the water or jump in with both feet. The choice is yours.

Take a step:

- Consider how much of your day is spent multitasking. Notice your level of productivity and stress. What insights can you gain?

- Approach each task with a single focus. Don't let yourself be distracted. What do you notice about your productivity and energy?

Test the water:

- What aspects of yourself are you avoiding or not wanting to see? Write down your fears and then ceremoniously burn and release them.

- What situations or events trigger your fight and flight response? How do you know you have been triggered? Write out steps you can take to not get triggered.

Jump in with both feet:

- When your fear or anxiety is elevated, become aware of what you are doing and notice your breathing. Feel the strong hormones and emotions flowing through your body. Sit quietly and watch them until they pass. Write down your experience and learnings.

- While meditating, notice times when strong emotions surface. Allow the emotions to pass through you and then consciously look underneath the emotions to identify what is going on below the surface.

Fostering a regular meditative practice

> *If you have time to breathe, you have time to meditate.*
> *You breathe when you walk. You breathe when you stand.*
> *You breathe when you lie down.*
> ~ Ajahn Amaro

Like any new skill or capability, it takes practice to learn how to meditate. Carving out time in our day for a regular, formal, seated practice in order to be present with our thoughts and emotions enables us to nurture peace and tranquility in our lives. Establishing a meditation practice typically begins with a short sitting period and grows into the continuous practice of observation and reflection. For many of us, there must be a perceived value or noticeable benefit to motivate us to develop a committed practice. Others of us are drawn to the ongoing self-discovery that occurs as the layers of our unconsciousness are peeled back. In deepening our meditation practice, it can be helpful to draw on the guidance and insight of seasoned meditator or a teacher. Either way, our sense of inner peace and contentment grows as our regular meditation practice unfolds.

Whenever we endeavour to learn a new skill, it takes time, patience and practice to cultivate proficiency. When we learned to walk for the first time, we had to develop our muscle strength, practice through trial and error, stumble and keep picking ourselves up. It took persistence and patience to eventually be able to walk without assistance or support. In our work, the skills we needed to reach our career goals included education and practical on-the-job experience. Learning to meditate is no exception and requires a consistent routine, commitment and persistence, in order to truly experience the benefits of meditation.

So many people sit to meditate for the first time and are surprised that they are not able to quiet their minds. If we took this approach of wanting to be an expert the first time we tried something, we would never really learn anything. One of the biggest mental challenges for meditators is understanding there is no goal to achieve in meditation. The key is getting out of our own way, letting go of setting goals and simply learning to be present with ourselves. For many of us, being alone with ourselves is the hardest obstacle of all, so we fill our time with distractions. It is ironic that we go about our lives setting goals and achieving results in order to feel a sense of inner contentment, when all we have to do is put down our distractions and be alone with ourselves in order to feel inner peace.

Part of the meditator's journey is to keep coming back to being present, again and again. By dropping the masks that we wear of our egocentric selves, we can simply be present in the here and now. There is no material possession, goal or job that can provide ongoing peace and contentment like the experience of being truly present in the moment. When we sit consistently to meditate, we begin the process of revealing our true nature to ourselves: a nature that is rich with bliss, peace and joy. Even the Buddha (meaning one who is awakened) practiced meditation in order to remove masks of ignorance, attachment and aversion. It is essential to remember that meditation is a practice. It is a practice we keep coming back to, without expectations, to simply experience a state of inner peace and contentment in every moment.

When we first begin to meditate, it is beneficial to practice a formal seated meditation for short intervals of time. Just like any new skill, we need to acclimate our mind and bodies to the experience before taking a more seasoned approach. If we wanted to free climb mountains, we would start with small cliffs to develop our skill and gain experience before attempting more difficult climbs. In the same way, when we sit for short periods of time, such as five to ten minutes, we allow our mind and body to become accustomed to a seated practice.

Finding a quiet place within our home to practice meditation is important. It is easy to be distracted when we are first learning to practice meditation, and this can bring up feelings of frustration. We can sit to meditate at any time during the day or evening. However, there are positive benefits to meditating early in the morning or during the evening hours. These times of the day tend to be less active as the people around us are either sleeping or settling down for the night. With less distraction and busyness, we are better able to be present to observe our thoughts. Early mornings have an added advantage because we feel renewed from our sleep and our minds are both more alert and quieter than at other times of the day.

As our meditative practice grows, we naturally increase our seated time to twenty-plus minutes and may sit during the morning and evening hours. As with any new habit, it is important to find the right time and location to nurture your practice. Equally important is the ability to let go of goals, as they relate to meditating. By simply practicing being present in each moment and letting our meditation practice unfold, we will experience a greater sense of peace and tranquility. Alternatively, you could also join a meditation group to promote a regular meditation practice and learn from a community of like-minded people.

Meditation does not just occur when we are seated in our formal practice. Meditation occurs in each and every moment we are conscious enough to be aware of ourselves. When we are walking, talking, cooking or working, can we be aware of ourselves performing these tasks? Can we be aware of our inhalation and exhalation with each step that we take when we are walking? Do we notice if our thoughts are in the past, present or future? Meditation is happening whenever we are the conscious witness to this very moment.

Thich Nhat Hanh uses a very simple yet mindful practice of noticing the inhale and exhale as he performs a walking meditation. A gatha (a mindfulness verse) that he teaches and uses to help practitioners be present during walks or in any moment of conscious awareness is as follows:

> Breathing in, I know I am breathing in.
> Breathing out, I know I am breathing out.[24]

So, regardless of what we are doing, meditation occurs in each moment we are in the observation of ourselves. This is the meditator's journey: to practice always being in the now and observing with conscious awareness. As each moment connects to the next moment and the next, we begin to develop a continuous stream of wakeful mindfulness. Through this practice, our inner peace and contentment grow. We are less focused on achieving or obtaining and more focused on being. When we are able to let go of striving, we can relax into the bliss of the present moment. Things that seemed so important and urgent hold less significance. To live in a constant state of self-awareness is to live with enlightenment. Our formal, seated meditation is dedicated

---

[24] *Present Moment Wonderful Moment*, Thich Nhat Hanh, The Corporation of the Buddha Educational Foundation, copyright 1990

time to practice observing the present moment, so we can be more present throughout all our daily activities.

There are benefits to practicing meditation, even if it is just for five minutes a day. Anytime we are aware of our breath flowing in and out of our body, it is time well spent. When we take a few minutes to let go of our thoughts of the past and the future, we are creating moments of peace within ourselves. Many people say they do not have time for a meditative practice. Yet, we can find time to get our morning cup of coffee. We can find time to play a round of golf. The issue is not about finding time but prioritizing it.

We must see and experience the benefit of meditation in order to establish a consistent, committed practice. Some people seek out meditation as a result of a traumatic or life changing experience in their life. For others, they intuitively feel drawn to meditation. Regardless of the reason, everyone who meditates benefits from the experience. Seasoned meditators experientially know the value of a consistent practice. They have developed their ability to gaze inwards for clarity and insight. Regular meditators have witnessed their inner storms and periods of serenity and still accept and love themselves, without judgement. They have become more at peace with themselves and the endless winds of change that we call life. Their meditation practice is the beacon that keeps them returning home to self and the bliss of inner peace.

A meditation teacher can be a helpful guide to help us navigate the twists, turns and deceptions we may face along the way. Deceptions can cause a meditator to falsely believe they have achieved a heighted level of awareness or that they know the true nature of reality. There are always more subtle layers of consciousness to be discovered and the belief that one has arrived if fraught with self-deception. As with any skill, the experience of someone who has learned the craft and knows the path can save a novice time and effort. Over the centuries, meditators have handed down their knowledge and insight to be shared with others who wish to embark on the meditator's journey.

A meditation teacher can establish the right foundation and understanding to get us started on the path. They can challenge our unconscious assumptions and break up our belief systems that would otherwise take us down a more difficult road. In choosing a teacher, we must be cognizant of finding someone we are drawn to and someone who is humble in their own practice. Remember that teachers are also students. They may have insight about the meditator's journey but they are still walking their own path. It is said that a master is someone who has learned to be a masterful student and someone who continues to look deeper into the truth of existence. Our teachers point us in the right direction, but we are the ones who must walk the path and learn from our own insights. The Buddha understood this, as we can see in the following passage from the Kalama Sutra, written so many centuries ago:

Do not believe, just because a wise man says so.
Do not believe, just because it has always been that way.
Do not believe, just because others may believe so.
Examine and experience for yourself.

Here are some suggested guidelines for you to consider when searching for a teacher:

1. Look for someone who calls to your spirit like a bee is drawn to a fragrant flower.

2. Find someone you can commit to spending a good amount of time with, such as a year(s). To go deep into your practice, it is important to spend enough time with your teacher. Otherwise, you may only get a sample of what could be offered.

3. Seek someone who models wisdom and compassion. A teacher who only has a conceptual understanding of higher consciousness will not be able to point you in the right direction for your own experiential growth, so do not assume someone is enlightened just because they say so. Look to have a positive, energetic experience in their presence.

4. Avoid someone who is looking for large sums of money in exchange for your enlightenment. There are always operating costs in a spiritual community or Ashram. However, you should not have to give up all your wealth to receive the teachings.

5. Avoid someone who is attempting to control you or others. If there are restrictions to your mobility or spiritual exploration, carefully consider if they are the right teacher for you. If they are abusive toward you or others, they are not the right teacher.

6. Avoid teachers who hold extremist views, such as that following their teachings are the right and only way. Be cautious of teachers who hold themselves with high regard over others. Be wary of teachers who have an egocentric perspective.

7. Always ask yourself, "Is it true?" From your experience, is it true what the teacher is offering? Do not blindly accept what is being offered as true. It is always wise to explore the truth within yourself

and then with your teacher. If an inquisitive mind is not welcome, perhaps the teacher is not the right one for you.

Practical application

To apply what you have learned in this section, try one or two of the suggestions below. Take a step, test the water or jump in with both feet. The choice is yours.

Take a step:

- Be aware of yourself as you walk or are out in nature. Notice your breathing, follow your inhalation and exhalation. Observe the sense of peace that surfaces from within.

- Notice when your thoughts are of the past or future. See if you can bring your focus back to the present moment. What do you experience in the present moment?

Test the water:

- Practice noticing your breathing during work meetings or conversations with friends. Feel how it brings you back to the present moment. What do you notice in the present moment?

- Practice meditation for five to ten minutes, three times per week.

Jump in with both feet:

- Establish a consistent meditation practice. Begin by sitting for five to ten minutes each day, preferably in the morning or evening. Use an App (e.g., Insight Timer) to help you create a consistent practice and to connect with other meditators.

- Join a local mediation group or take some meditation classes from a skilled teacher.

Meditative practice

The mind is susceptible to suggestions.
It learns whatever you teach it.
~ Swami Brahmananda

Finding a quiet place to meditate daily, preferably in the same location in your home, creates a meditative space for you to return to each time you meditate. Having a consistent location to meditate will quickly entrain the mind and body to know that this is where you sit to be still and present. Keeping some special mementos or sacred objects in this location will also help to reinforce the sanctity of your meditation space. In addition, by using the same space for each meditation session, the energy in the room becomes more meditative. We probably all have examples of times in our lives when we walked into a room and felt the energy in the space. Perhaps it is walking into a meeting room and feeling the tension. Maybe it is the feeling you get when you walk into a sacred place, such as a church or a temple, and notice how quiet and still the room feels. Creating a quiet and peaceful meditative space encourages you to slow down and feel calm whenever you are in the room. Our mind and body then settle more easily, and we are able to be present with ourselves.

Given our busy lives with other family members around us, it may be challenging to dedicate a room or space for meditation. Choosing meditation times when family is asleep or away can help in creating a quiet space to meditate. Another option is to put out your sacred objects each time you meditate somewhere in your home, creating a ceremony or moment of centering before you meditate.

You can also meditate on your patio, in your yard, a nearby park or the woods. Choose any location that calls to you where you are able to sit quietly with yourself and be the witness to each moment. As we meditate, peace settles over us like a soft mist over our lake of consciousness. We become the witness to each moment and are filled with contentment.

Our posture during meditation is important too. A seated posture cultivates alignment of our physical bodies with our mind, allowing us to settle more quickly into our meditative practice. If we are physically uncomfortable during meditation, it will be difficult to sit still and be observant. It can be helpful to do some form of physical movement or exercise before sitting to meditate. Practicing yoga in advance of meditating is a great way to prepare the body for longer periods of sitting. Walking or stretching before meditation are also ways to settle the body.

While seated postures will vary among meditation traditions, most agree there are six posture points important to a formal seated meditation:

1. Lower extremities (in seated position on floor or chair)

    The traditional way to practice meditation is in a seated position on the floor. Legs are crossed with feet resting comfortably on the floor or alongside the calves and shins. However, this traditional posture can be challenging for people with tight hips and knee problems.

    Alternatively, you can sit on a chair with good back support. In this scenario, your knees are comfortably bent at a ninety-degree angle and your feet are flat on the floor. Sitting in a comfortable position will allow you to quickly settle into your meditation and be less distracted by your physical body.

2. Hips (level and supported)

   Its best to have your hips level and supported by a cushion, if on the floor, or in a comfortable chair, if seated. Ideally, your hips should be higher than your knees, which will help to keep your spine in its natural curvature.

3. Spine (straight, and supported if necessary)

   Keeping your spine long and erect will help in the flow of energy from the base of the spine all the way up to the base of the skull. Your spine is like the circuit board for your body. Electrical current flows through your nervous system from the brain to the various parts of the body. When you sit to meditate, the energy within your body slows down and your brainwaves decelerate. Keeping your spine straight during meditation will allow for the free flow of energy up and down the spine. Ideally, you would sit on a cushion or chair, with a straight spine. However, this may be challenging for longer periods of time for new meditators. Using a back support can be helpful until you are able to sit with your spine straight for extended periods.

   Note: In the early stages, some people fall asleep during meditation. When your energy slows down, there can be times when your body is unable to accommodate your slower level of vibration. A good analogy is to compare this to what happens with the electrical breakers in our homes. When the energy flow fluctuates or surges in your home, you can blow a breaker that will have to be reset. A similar process can occur within your body when your energy slows down, and your body needs to reboot to adjust to the new energy flow. This is when you temporarily fall asleep. Continuing to practice meditation will allow your body to acclimate to this slower energy and be able to integrate it without falling asleep.

4. Arms and hands (relaxed)

Your arms can be relaxed along the sides of your body with your hands either resting comfortably on your thighs or placed one on top of the other in your lap. If you are resting your hands on your thighs, the palms can either be face down or up. Palms down will be more focused on keeping energy within the body. Palms up will be more focused on receiving energy and being open. Some people use a hand mudra (one of the symbolic hand gestures used in religious ceremonies and dances of India and in yoga [25]) such as pressing the tip of the index finger and thumb together. Using a mudra is optional and can be incorporated whenever you feel so inclined.

5. Jaw and mouth (relaxed)

The jaw and mouth are relaxed. Typically, your mouth remains closed during meditation and breathing is done through the nose. However, exhaling out your

---

[25] Merriam-Webster Dictionary

mouth for a few initial breaths is a great way to let go of stress and tension within the body and can be a good way to start your meditation.

6. Eyes (open or closed)

There are different schools of thought on whether you should meditate with your eyes open or closed. Meditating with your eyes closed focuses the mind inward. This approach has often been thought of as the traditional way to meditate. Some find it helpful in calming the mind as there is then no external visual stimuli. This approach can lead to daydreaming by indulging the thoughts that surface in the mind. However, for new meditators, it may be beneficial to meditate with your eyes closed to strengthen your ability to remain focused.

An open-eyed meditation helps develop the skill of being able to observe the mind while being present in the every day world. You learn not to be distracted by external stimuli while remaining observant of your thoughts. However, you can also become focused on external factors that can fill your mind. Some schools of thought suggest the eyes should remain open and not blink during meditation. This can be especially challenging for new meditators and thus may be a practice that develops over time.

Consistently using the six posture points during seated meditation will reinforce a strong meditation practice and allow you to settle into meditation quickly and easily. Keeping your meditation to shorter times in the early stages will allow your body to become accustomed to sitting and will build up your internal strength to sit for longer periods of time without back support.

To help you in creating a regular practice refer to the Guidelines for Establishing a Meditative Practice at the end of this section.

Practical application

To apply what you have learned in this section, try one or two of the suggestions below. Take a step, test the water or jump in with both feet. The choice is yours.

Take a step:

- Sit in a quiet place for five to ten minutes every few days to meditate.

- Practice sitting with back support until you are able to sit comfortably on your own for twenty minutes or more away from the wall or chairback.

Test the water:

- Find a quiet space in your home to sit and meditate daily using the six posture points of meditation practice.

- Keep practicing despite the fact that you may fall asleep at times or feel discouraged. Know that you are making progress as you are able to sit wakefully for longer periods of time. The judgements we hold about our meditations are simply judgements, nothing more.

Jump in with both feet:

- Create a separate space in your home for daily meditations. Place your sacred objects in the room. Clear the energy in the room by smudging it with sage, sounding a bell/chime or playing meditation music for twenty-four hours before sitting.

- Keep a journal about your meditative experiences. Reflect on how your meditation has progressed over time.

Meditation techniques

> *Like the state of space, the mind transcends thought.*
> *Set it at ease in its own nature, without*
> *rejecting it or maintaining it.*
> ~Tilopa

There are numerous forms of meditation used throughout the world, including Vedic, Vipassana (a form of meditation in the Theravadin Buddhist tradition), Zen, and Transcendental. Each of these forms has evolved over the centuries. And most forms of meditation have an object of focus that allows the mind to both settle and return to when distractions arise.

The mind is designed to think. That is its job.[26] When we meditate, the mind continues to be busy, so having a focus gives the mind the task of coming back to an object of focus. There are a number of focus methodologies used in meditation. Some of the more common ones are using the breath or a mantra (i.e., a word or sound repeated to aid concentration in meditation[27]), focusing on the space between the eyebrows (often referred to as the third eye) or a mandala (a circular figure representing the universe in Hindu and Buddhist symbolism [28]), or gazing at a lit candle.

In the Western world, meditation practice often has been contemporized into categorizes of silent, guided or mindfulness. All of these practices have methods to slow us

---

[26] YouTube, Train Your Monkey Mind, Yongey Mingyur Rinpoche, September 8,2016 https://www.youtube.com/watch?v=lt9OcLynjwE
[27] English Oxford Living Dictionaries
[28] English Oxford Living Dictionaries

down in the pursuit of exploring self and the true nature of existence, resulting in greater inner peace and tranquility.

Throughout history, meditative practices have been offered by religious scholars and mystics to raise humankind's consciousness and to provide a practical approach to self-exploration and discovery. I have provided a brief summary of some of these meditative practices below, but by no means is this a comprehensive list.

Vedic – Originated over 5,000 years ago in India out of the practices of the Brahmin priests. This form of meditation is an effortless meditation in which the meditator silently repeats a sound mantra to gently focus the mind. As the mantra sound softens, the meditator rests his/her mind in the simple observation of whatever surfaces. Some have referred to this technique as the householder practice as it provides a practical approach for non-monastics.[29]

Vipassana –This practice, based upon the original teachings of the Buddha, originated about 2,500 years ago in India and was viewed as a remedy for universal ills. Vipassana means "to see things as they are." The focus is initially on the breath, and then shifts to more and more subtle awareness of the body and the mind. [30]

Buddhist – This meditative practice is based on the teachings of the Buddha from over 2,500 years ago. The teachings, which have been preserved in ancient Buddhist

---

[29] Meditation Plex, The Vedic Mediation Technique Explained, http://www.meditationplex.com/vedic-meditation/vedic-meditation-technique-explained/

[30] Vipassana Mediation, S.N. Goenka https://www.dhamma.org/en/index

texts, are passed down and added to through teacher-to-student transmissions.[31] The focus is on the observation of the breath and the insight gained from the exploration of the mind. Buddhist philosophy helps to understand and explain the intricacies of our mind and human thought.

Zen – A form of Buddhism founded in China about 1,500 years ago and imported to Japan in the thirteenth century. Zen meditation either uses the breath as a focus or simply rests the mind in the present moment.[32] The use of a koan (a paradoxical anecdote or riddle without a solution)[33] is another technique used to help focus and still the mind.

Transcendental – This meditation practice is based on the teachings of Maharishi Mahesh Yogi and was first introduced in India around 1950 and more recently in North America. Transcendental meditation uses a sound or word mantra given to a student by their teacher. The practitioner silently repeats the mantra a few times and then observes the mind. When the meditator notices they have become caught up in thought, they once again repeat the mantra a few times and return to noticing the mind.

As previously stated, a meditation practice typically begins with an object of focus, especially for new meditators, to help in directing the mind's attention. The object of focus can vary among the different meditative practices or a combination of techniques may be used. A common

---

[31] sensAgent Dictionary, Buddhist Meditation http://dictionary.sensagent.com/Buddhist_meditation/en-en/
[32] Live and Dare, Types of Meditation, by Giovanni, January 28, 2015 https://liveanddare.com/types-of-meditation
[33] English Oxford Living Dictionaries

and practical object of focus is the breath. It is always present, never needs to be acquired and does not need to be handed down from teacher to student. As one settles into meditation, the mind's focus is placed on the inhalation and the exhalation. The meditator watches as the breath comes in and goes out. When the mind wanders, the meditator notices and re-establishes the focus on the breath. A key component to this practice is to not judge the wandering mind. Chogyam Trungpa Rinpoche instructed his students to silently say "thinking"[34] whenever they noticed their mind had wandered and to then come back to observing the breath. In this way, there is no judgement or criticism of oneself when the mind gets distracted. The practice becomes the continual returning to the observation of one's breath. When consistently using this practice, the mind and the body transcend everyday awareness and the meditator experiences a deep sense of peace and tranquility.

The use of a mantra is another tool to help meditators focus the mind during meditation. Since the mind's role is to think, giving it a specific repetitive task helps to entrain the mind to focus. In the East, mantras are traditionally in Sanskrit, an ancient language of India dating back more than 3,500 years. One of the most well-known mantras is OM, a sacred sound in most Eastern religions and a frequently used mantra in the Vedic tradition. In the Buddhist tradition a common mantra is "Om Mani Padme Hum" and in the Hindu tradition "Om Namah Shivaya." Mantras are not restricted to Eastern religions. One of the common ones

---

[34] When things fall apart: Heart Advice for Difficult Times, Pema Chodron, Shambhala Publications, 2005

used in the Christian tradition is "Ave Maria" and "Allah Akbar" in the Islamic tradition.

Within the Transcendental meditation practice, a unique mantra is confidentially given by the teacher to the student. Just like using the breath as a focus, a mantra is silently repeated by the meditator and re-established when the mind wanders. A mantra is usually used for an extended period of time (e.g. months or years) and may even be used for one's whole lifetime.

Another object of focus during meditation is the space between the eyebrows, referred to as the third eye, a point on the forehead corresponding to one of the chakras in yoga, often depicted as an eye and associated with enlightenment or mystical insight.[35] A meditator places the mind's attention on the third eye as a focus point. As with other objects of focus, when the mind wanders the meditator redirects attention back to the third eye. A common approach in using the third eye focus is to visualize one's inhalation and exhalation occurring at the location of the third eye.

There are a couple of focus techniques that are specific to open eyed meditations, such as gazing at a mandala or a lit candle. In Hindu and Buddhist symbolism, a Mandala is a circular figure representing the universe.[36] One of the most ancient mandalas is the Shri Yantra Mandala, illustrated below (Image 2).

---

[35] Your Dictionary
[36] English Oxford Living Dictionaries

Image 2 - Shri Yantra Mandala

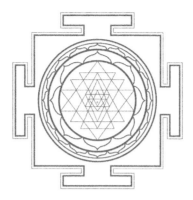

For this practice, one sits in front of the mandala gazing at it with eyes open. This practice is done without blinking. Through the gazing process, the mind focuses on the mandala, which eventually disappears as the image is superimposed on the retina. There is also spiritual symbolism contained within a mandala. The geometric design is a representation of universal manifestation. All manifestations are creations from the central source of consciousness, as illustrated by a point in the centre of the mandala.

The practice of gazing continuously at a lit candle as one's object of focus is a similar approach to enhance a meditator's ability to concentrate. With practice, a meditator can relax their focus on the candle without blinking or tearing. Just like mandala gazing, the lit candle eventually disappears as the observer (subject) and the observed (object) merge into one. Both these techniques take commitment and continuous practice and are best suited for meditators under the guidance of a meditation teacher.

A more common approach to the open-eyed meditation is placing one's gaze on the floor, two to three feet in-front of you. Just as one does with a mandala or lit candle, the eyes remain open without blinking. The gaze is soft, not really focusing on anything, but rather being in the observation of whatever surfaces in the mind. When the mind wanders, the meditator simply comes back to the open space in front of them. All of these meditation techniques energetically slow us down and allow us to experience deeper states of inner peace and calm.

In the West, we have contemporized these meditation traditions into non-sectarian practices. We have used the term silent meditation to describe a more traditional practice that is done in silence. Meditators may use the breath or silent mantra as a focus point, but there is no chanting or sound used as part of the practice. Another example is the guided meditation. In this practice the meditator is guided through a visualization process by a teacher or instructor. The focus is the visualization that is used to create a sense of inner peace and calm. The guided visualization can focus on being in nature or feeling the stress and tension leaving the body. A meditator may also use their inner focus to provide their own guided meditation. In this way, there is no reliance on an external guide.

Mindfulness meditation is a combination of Buddhist and Vipassana techniques. It was established in the West in the 1970s. In mindfulness meditation, the practitioner focuses their attention on the breath.[37] The intention is to

---

[37] Live and Dare, Types of Meditation, by Giovanni, January 28, 2015 https://liveanddare.com/types-of-meditation

just notice so as to be mindful of whatever surfaces without adding anything to it.

As you can see, there are many varied approaches to the practice of meditation. People are able to select a path that speaks to them. While there are many paths, they all lead to the same place of greater inner peace and serenity. A key element of a regular meditation practice is committing to one form of practice and staying with it for a substantial period of time, such as months or years. Just as our mind wanders, we can move from technique to technique never going deep enough to really experience the benefits of our practice. Meditation becomes a commitment to discovering inner truth and liberation from the limiting perspective we hold about ourselves and reality. Inner peace and contentment are the by-product of a committed mediation practice. As we practice meditation, we more readily see the fluctuations that occur in the dance of dynamic peace.

Practical application

To apply what you have learned in this section, try one or two of the suggestions below. Take a step, test the water or jump in with both feet. The choice is yours.

Take a step:

- Sit quietly while listening to a guided on-line mediation. Use a Google search to locate a free sample.

- Sit quietly while listing to mediation music, such as "Bliss-Music" by Kip Mazuy (http://www.bliss-music.com/).

Test the water:

- Try meditating using a mantra (e.g., Om Namah Shivaya). Notice your experience.

- Try meditating by simply observing your inhalation and exhalation. Notice your experience.

Jump in with both feet:

- Commit to one meditation technique for a period of time (such as six months to a year). Observe how your practice changes over time.

- Join a regular mediation group.

Being present

> *Like the sun and the moon,*
> *meditate in brightness and clarity!*
> ~ Milarepa

Returning again and again to our meditation, we learn to be the witness to our thoughts, emotions and beliefs. We develop the ability to sit in moments of stillness and in the discomfort of our own selves. All the while, we slowly relinquish our ego and learn to love and accept ourselves as we are. Meditation practice creates the window through which we can experience being fully present with ourselves. We awaken to the here and now as we learn to be in the observation of ourselves moment to moment. There is a profound experience of expansion and awe in these moments of true presence. The past and the future do not exist in the wonderment of the present moment. We become more centered in the present, which is the only true existence. Through practice, surrender and self-love we find greater inner peace and happiness.

We keep returning to meditation so we can willingly pause to be aware of our thoughts and emotions as they unfold. We develop the ability to be with the beauty and the ugliness that we see within ourselves as we meditate. It is easy to be the witness to the positivity and splendour we observe within ourselves. When we are aware of our kindness, generosity and compassion, there is a sense of inner happiness and contentment. So often, we cling to our feelings of joy and happiness because we never want the pleasure to end. Yet, not unlike other thoughts and feelings, happiness is an impermanent experience, just like the passing clouds. When we try to hold onto pleasant feelings, we are left feeling disappointed as they eventually fall away like sand through our fingers.

The meditator's journey is to watch the coming and going of thoughts and emotions with detached observation, neither clinging to them nor pushing them away. When we are aware of our clinging, we need to look underneath this feeling to explore what our grasping is about. We may notice that these feelings are the by-product of a hidden agenda that has caused us to act. Perhaps our compassion has been given in the hope of acknowledgment or recognition. We may be attached to a specific outcome which creates suffering for us when it does not materialize. Compassion given freely without attachment brings inner peace and joy. Compassion given to obtain something breeds suffering.

In the same way, we become quite uncomfortable when we are confronted with having to sit in our simmering emotions of fear, anger, jealousy or hatred. The intensity of our emotions can make us want to escape from ourselves. At times we may feel as though we have just been sprayed by a skunk and cannot get the smell off no matter how hard we try. At these times, our thoughts and emotions may be so strong that we are unable to sit still or we lash out at others. Meditation practice prepares us to be able to be with ourselves in these more challenging times. Our practice enables us to come back to witnessing our thoughts rather than jumping on them with intensity. We are able to step back from the churning feelings and look underneath to see what held beliefs are causing our anguish. Perhaps our spouse has made a comment that brings up hurt feelings. We can react by instantly erupting into emotions of anger or frustration. Our suffering is not in the act but the arising thoughts about the act. The comments made by our spouse incite thoughts that ramp up with a fervor, such as "What did he mean when he said that?" or "She knows that upsets me."

Through our practice, we remain open to whatever comes to us, and as a result, are better able to respond with open curiosity. Our meditation practice enables us to pause and observe our thoughts that say, "It should be other than it is." We become less reactive and more inquisitive about what life presents to us in each moment. Through our regular meditative practice, we are better able to be in our own stew of thoughts and emotions with an exposed calmness.

As a result of meditation, our ability to be accepting of ourselves during both good and difficult times grows. Our inner lighthouse becomes the witness to whatever is unfolding, and we are less swayed by judgements one way or the other. We learn to accept ourselves when we feel happy and when we feel down. Many people hold the belief that a seasoned meditator does not feel emotions as strongly as a non-meditator. The experience is the same except that over time the intensity diminishes. It is as though you have seen yourself in all states and you have learned to accept and love yourself regardless. A meditator learns to unravel the story going on behind the scenes and truthfully acknowledge with compassion the humanness of each moment. We learn to be present with ourselves regardless of the circumstances. We accept our feelings of sorrow and joy with the same watchful acknowledgement. Meditation always brings us back to the present moment. We are able let go of the past as a history that we cannot change and to recognize our thoughts of the future as illusory fantasies. As Pema Chodron says, "All we have is this very moment."[38] When we are able to remain the observer, we feel a great sense of inner peace and calm. Like the willow tree, we are easily blown by the winds of change and yet remain solidly grounded in the here and now.

When we experience being in the present moment, we feel expansiveness and awe simultaneously. Time seems to stand still, if only for a second, and we are profoundly moved by the weight of this very moment. There is a sense of bliss and peace that fills our body. Each of us has experienced these moments in our lives. Perhaps it occurred during the rising of a full moon. Maybe it was the moment when fresh snow sparkled as the sun's rays reached out and touched it. Possibly it was the sound of a symphony playing Ode to Joy.

In the quiet stillness it can seem as if an eternity has passed. It is in these moments that we experience our true nature, one of universal consciousness and peace. The petty issues of every day life seem infinitesimal and unimportant. Our spirits are lifted as we have a glimpse into our soul. In the here and now, the past and the future are inconceivable. We have touched the present moment where peace and tranquility envelope us like a warm blanket. Through our meditative practice, we keep returning to the present moment. We learn to focus our thoughts and feelings on those things that bring us joy and peace. We see the joy in the ordinary and are less interested in the trappings of the external world. Meditation is our tool to help us remember our divine nature and to remove the veil to inner peace and tranquility.

---

[38] When things fall apart: Heart Advice for Difficult Times, Pema Chodron, Shambhala Publications, 2005

Over the next two sections, we will explore various aspects of our daily lives that either pull us toward or push us away from greater peace. Each topic is another layer that when explored and peeled away provides greater insight into ourselves and leads to greater inner peace.

Practical application

To apply what you have learned in this section, try one or two of the suggestions below. Take a step, test the water or jump in with both feet. The choice is yours.

Take a step:

- Sitting quietly, watch your thoughts surface and pass like clouds.

- Notice times when you are creating a storyline to a situation or event. Is the story true? How do you know it is true?

Test the water:

- Notice when you are trying to hold on to moments of happiness and joy. What is it you are clinging to? Can you simply be in the observation of happiness without attachment?

- Notice when you are trying to push away or ignore moments of unhappiness and suffering. What is it that you are trying to avoid? Can you be in the observation of your suffering without commentary?

Jump in with both feet:

- Catch yourself in moments of reactivity. What is it that you are reacting to? What is the underlying belief that you have? Is there an expected outcome that you are not seeing?

- Practice being in the acceptance of what is. When you cannot accept what is, notice the underlying belief or perspective that is causing you to suffer.

Guidelines for Establishing a Meditative Practice

The following guidelines, will help you establish a regular meditative practice:

1. Find or create a place within your home where you can regularly meditate. Ideally, use a separate room in your home. A corner of a quiet room, a corner in your bedroom or a quiet space in your basement will also work.

2. Let others in your home know what you are doing and make any requests of them so they can support you in your practice. For example, have quiet time in your home as you meditate or have others leave you alone while you meditate.

3. Place some personal objects in the space where you meditate that will remind you that it is a place of meditation. A book of poems or quotes, a picture of an inspirational teacher, some fresh flowers or a candle are just a few ideas.

4. Determine the best time for you to meditate during the day when you will not be interrupted. It might be early in the morning, after everyone has left for the day or perhaps in the evening before bed.

5. Commit to meditating for at least five to ten minutes each time you sit to meditate. Over time, let your meditation periods lengthen as you become better able to sit for longer periods.

6. Use a timer or meditation app to set up a meditation time (e.g., ten minutes). In doing so you can focus your awareness on your meditation without constantly wondering if the time is up.

7. Commit to meditating regularly, at least three or more times a week. Increase the number of days as you feel comfortable. You may even want to meditate a couple of times per day (e.g., morning and evening) as your practice develops.

8. As you prepare to sit for meditation, practice the six postural points of a seated meditation.

9. Use an object of focus during your meditation, such as your breath. Return again and again to being aware of your inhalation and exhalation whenever you notice that your mind has wandered during your meditative practice.

10. After your meditation, sit for a few minutes to notice your meditation experience and how you are feeling (e.g., calm, restless, peaceful, etc.).

11. You may want to consider exploring different types of meditation (e.g., Vedic, Vipassana, Zen, etc.) to select the format that will work best for you.

12. Some individuals like to keep a daily meditation journal in which they document their experiences. This can be a great tool to reflect on how your meditation experience has shifted over time.

13. Consider joining a meditation group to support you in establishing a regular practice. It can be helpful

to share and discuss your experiences with others on a similar journey.

14. Recognize that each day is a new meditative experience. Some days may be quiet and peaceful. On other days your mind may be busy or you may feel restless. Throughout it all, continually return to your object of focus and remain the witness to whatever is unfolding.

15. Remember that meditation is the observation of what is. Whatever is surfacing or happening in your meditation, your only responsibility is to notice what is unfolding with non-judgement and a detached witnessing.

Chapter Four: Creating peace in our life

Peace will come to the hearts of men

when they realize their oneness with the universe.

It is everywhere.

~Black Elk

Do no harm

*Nonviolence requires much more courage
than violence.*
~ Mahatma Gandhi

In Eastern philosophies and religions there is the cardinal virtue of ahimsa, which means to cause no injury or harm. The word is derived from Hindu and Buddhist doctrines of refraining from harming any living being.[39] In creating greater peace of mind, our actions toward ourselves and all living beings play a key role. We cannot separate ourselves from the earth, animals, plants and insects. We are all living beings. Causing harm to one has an impact on all. The actions we take, the thoughts we nurture and the feelings we hold affect how we interact with others. Treating all life forms with loving-kindness and compassion has a direct bearing on our own level of inner peace. At the same time, the words, thoughts, feelings and actions we bring toward ourselves either increase or decrease our own experience of inner contentment. When we are loving and compassionate toward ourselves, our capacity to be kind and caring toward others increases. Similarly, our perceptions of and reactions to how others treat us can also impact our state of inner peace. The more we allow others to influence our thinking about ourselves and others, the greater the impact on our internal peace. Fostering inner harmony is created by treating all living beings and ourselves in a way that does not cause harm.

---

[39] Merriam-Webster Dictionary

The Zen Buddhist master and peace activist Thich Nhat Hanh has written and spoken about the concept of interbeing, which is the interconnectedness of all phenomenon. In his discourses on interbeing, Thich Nhat Hanh illustrates with profound simplicity the perspective that all phenomenon is connected and that no-thing can exist in isolation. To explain his point, Thich Nhat Hanh uses the example of a cloud being in a single piece of paper:

> If you are a poet, you will see clearly that there is a cloud floating in this sheet of paper. Without a cloud, there will be no rain; without rain, the trees cannot grow: and without trees, we cannot make paper. The cloud is essential for the paper to exist. If the cloud is not here, the sheet of paper cannot be here either. So, we can say that the cloud and the paper inter-are *(interbeing)*.[40]

The paper cannot exist without the cloud, the tree and all the things and people that go into making the paper. The tree needs all of the elements provided by the universe in order to grow (the sun, the cloud, the rain, the soil, etc.). Each of these elements is contained within a single piece of paper. Without humans to cut down the tree and make the paper, the paper would not exist. This very simple illustration points to the interconnectedness of all phenomenon. Humans too could not exist without the universe, the sun, the earth and the rain. We could not

---

[40] *Interbeing: Fourteen Guidelines for Engaged Buddhism* (Parallax Press, 1987)

exist without our parents, and their parents and all of our ancestors that came before them. We tend to think about our existence in isolation from everything and everyone. But in truth, we could not exist without all phenomenon that came before to enable our existence.

Consider the scientific evidence today of global warming and the impact we are having on the earth. If we cut down the Amazon rainforest, it has an impact on the rest of the world. The earth's warming climate has an impact on the glaciers and sea levels. No-thing exists in isolation from the rest of all phenomenon. Thus, how we interact with the rest of existence has a direct bearing on us and our level of inner peace.

Not causing harm begins with how we think, feel, and act toward ourselves. The thoughts we harbour about ourselves either increase or decrease our inner harmony. If our thoughts are that we are unworthy of love or acceptance, we will be unable to develop a sense of inner contentment. In some cases, the thoughts we have about ourselves can be quite harsh and negative. We may repeatedly tell ourselves we have failed, or that we do not deserve to be happy. We mentally beat ourselves up if we have made a mistake or have done something that we perceive to be wrong. Repetitive negative thinking pulls us further away from the experience of inner peace.

At the same time, the thoughts we have about ourselves can be conscious as well as unconscious. We may be consciously aware of our thoughts, noticing which ones are negative and which ones are positive. In this situation, it can be easy to catch ourselves saying negative things in our minds and to stop these habitual patterns. However, there are many thoughts that are so engrained into our consciousness that they run automatically. We do not hear the words we say to ourselves. For some, the words we tell ourselves may be so harsh that we would not say them out loud to another person. Yet, if we want to create greater inner peace, we must not only hear our thoughts but begin to challenge their validity.

The first step in discovering which stories we are telling ourselves is by being aware that there is in fact a story playing out in our minds, such as "I am unworthy." The next step is to ask ourselves whether it is true. We need to begin reframing our thoughts so they are kind, compassionate and loving. Inner peace can only be experienced when we are accepting of ourselves with all of our perceived flaws and shortcomings. It is not that we do not want to see the truth about ourselves. Rather we want to see the truth and still be able to treat ourselves with loving-kindness and compassion.

In some cases, our negative thinking can be so intense that we can be physically harmful to ourselves. Over the centuries, humans have found numerous ways to cause themselves harm. We may deprive ourselves of food or drink to look a certain way or to address our inner feelings of shame. We may inflict physical harm on our bodies as a form of coping with the strong emotions and feelings we have about ourselves. There are recent historical accounts within some religions of individuals flagellating themselves as a form of penance for not being worthy enough or as a way to control desire.

The pain of negative emotions is still as prevalent today as it was in earlier times. While some situations of physical harm are more obvious, such as anorexia and bulimia, others may be not as evident such as alcoholism and drug addiction. To find inner peace, we must be willing to face our innermost pain and suffering. In this context, pain is of the body and suffering is of the mind. Our pain is the physical sensations of a toothache, arthritis, a broken leg or recovery after surgery. Suffering is a result of the thoughts we harbour that cause us anguish, anxiety, heartbreak or stress. We need to recognize the ways we are causing ourselves harm and consciously learn to accept all aspects of ourselves with love and compassion. There is a great deal of courage required to not only be willing to see our inner suffering but also to begin to challenge our thinking and feelings in order to heal and find greater self-acceptance.

From the perspective that all existence is interconnected, the degree to which we foster and create inner peace has a direct correlation with how we treat all other living beings. The thoughts and feelings we hold about life determine our actions, and these actions determine our internal contentment. We cannot experience inner peace while harbouring anger toward others. Our anger burns like an inner fire and our thoughts and feelings are the fuel that stoke that fire. We must be willing to recognize that our thoughts and feelings are creating inner storms. Only by turning inwardly to look at ourselves can we hope to create peace. By being willing to look at our own suffering, we find the compassion to see others' torment. Understanding and empathy grow along with a willingness to see the humanity of others. Being unconditionally empathetic and supportive of our fellow humans in finding their own inner peace has a positive impact on our own level of inner peace.

Harmony and contentment are not limited to human beings but extend to all life forms. Yongey Mingyur Rinpoche, in his book *The Joy of Living* writes, "Other sentient beings—people, animals and even insects—are just like us, that their basic motivation is to experience peace and to avoid suffering."[41] All living beings have an innate desire to experience joy, love, and peace. When we care for the earth and live in harmony with nature, we experience greater peace within ourselves. The extent to which we are loving and compassionate to all life forms has a direct impact on our ability to increase our own sense of self-love and compassion. When we care for all life, we are also innately caring for ourselves. Our spirits are lifted when we take action to clean up the oceans, replant the forests, and purify drinking water for all living beings. In caring for our environment, we are caring for all beings. Because of our interconnectedness, our inner peace corresponds to the level of kindness and compassion we show to all living beings around us.

In our interactions with others, our inner contentment can be influenced by how we let others treat us and how we respond. While we have no control over what others say or do, we do have control over the thoughts and feelings we harbour within ourselves. If we truly want inner peace, we must be selective with the seeds we water in our consciousness and those we choose to weed out. Similarly, carefully surrounding ourselves with people who are positive and supportive while removing ourselves from those who are negative and draining help us foster inner peace. Being selective of the people and situations we allow into our lives will have a direct bearing on our level of contentment. Thus, whenever possible, removing

---

[41] The Joy of Living, Unlocking the Secret & Science of Happiness, Yongey Mingyur Rinpoche, Three Rivers Press, NY 2007

ourselves from those people that would cause us harm will go a long way to the growth of our level of contentment. Unfortunately, being able to remove ourselves from harm may not always be possible. Yet, there are examples of individuals who have survived personal hardship as a result of their inner determination and conviction. During his twenty-seven years of incarceration, Nelson Mandela drew on a poem written by William Ernest Henley, entitled "Invictus" to give him strength and inspiration:

> Out of the night that covers me,
> Black as the pit from pole to pole,
> I thank whatever gods may be
> For my unconquerable soul.
>
> In the fell clutch of circumstance
> I have not winced nor cried aloud.
> Under the bludgeoning of chance
> My head is bloody, but unbowed.
>
> Beyond this place of wrath and tears
> Looms but the horror of the shade,
> And yet the menace of the years
> Finds, and shall find, me unafraid.
>
> It matters not how strait the gate,
> How charged with punishments the scroll.
> I am the master of my fate:
> I am the captain of my soul.

At the core of inner peace is this mindset of ahimsa (not causing harm) and in turn caring for all the myriad life forms. Yet, over the centuries, humans have felt a sense of dominance over the earth and all its inhabitants. We have acted as though humans can consume without regard for the earth, animals, plants or environment. We short-sightedly take whatever we want, whenever we want it, with little to no regard.

When the number of humans was small, the impact on the earth was minimal. As of 2018, the global human population is over 7.6 billion and growing.[42] Our impact on the earth is significant and profound. With few exceptions, we live in a world of discontent and disharmony. If our innate nature is based on a desire to live in peace and harmony, each of us plays a role in contributing to world peace. Still, if one takes the perspective of human dominance over the earth, do we not have a duty to care for the earth and all its inhabitants? Through our actions, words and deeds, we are promoting either global discontent or harmony. Is it unrealistic and utopian to think that humanity could live in peace and harmony with all life? Perhaps, however, each of us is a microcosm of the universal consciousness. When we foster inner peace, there are ripples throughout the consciousness of humanity.

Practical application

To apply what you have learned in this section, try one or two of the suggestions below. Take a step, test the water or jump in with both feet. The choice is yours.

---

[42] Worldometers Population, http://www.worldometers.info/world-population/

Take a step:

- Notice your negative thoughts and challenge yourself by asking, "Are they true?"
- Consider the interconnectedness of all life by recognizing the sun, rain, earth and air elements in all beings.

Test the water:

- In what way(s) do you harbour anger? Consider ways to release this anger. For example, write a letter to someone you feel anger towards, and then release it by burning it; speak to the person you are angry with in a way that is compassionate and kind.
- Seek professional help to deal with your anger.
- Let go of negative people or situations in your life. What do you notice when you a make this change?

Jump in with both feet:

- Look at ways you may be harming yourself (e.g., eating poorly, lack of exercise). Take one step to be more loving toward yourself. For example, make different food choices, walk or jog two or more times per week, reduce your alcohol consumption, change your negative self-talk.
- Listen to the negative storyline running through your mind when you are feeling down. Write down all the things you are grateful for in your life. Notice if your negativity shifts as a result of making a list.

Consumption

There are four types of consumption we will look explore: edible foods, sense impressions, volition and consciousness.

Edible Foods

> *Tell me what you eat
> and I will tell you who you are.*
> ~ Jean Anthelme Brillat-Savarin

Our inner peace is affected by everything we put into our bodies, including what we eat, how it is prepared and how we consume it. Most diets around the world have meat as a key staple. Yet, the way we raise, treat and slaughter animals for human consumption is often done in the most inhumane way. As consumers, we are sanitized from this atrocious treatment of animals as we shop the grocery store isles selecting nicely wrapped packages of prepared meats. In full disclosure, I have been a vegetarian for over thirty years. This lighter diet has both enhanced my meditation experience and supported the humane treatment of animals.

The energy we put into our food as we prepare it for consumption also impacts our state of contentment. If a meal is prepared with anger or strong emotion, the food is energized with the same energy. A meal prepared with care, compassion and love will create a more joyous feeling for the person eating the meal. Once prepared, the way in which we eat our meal adds to our sense of inner tranquility. When we are conscious and acknowledge what we are eating, our sense of joy increases. Some recent research suggests that a vegetarian diet can significantly reduce our greenhouse gas emissions, reduce global mortality rates and decrease health care costs.[43] We are a part of all life. How we treat and consume nourishment has a direct bearing on our own level of contentment and inner peace.

Everything we consume has given of itself in order that we may survive. The water we drink and the plants and animals we eat provide our bodies with all the sustenance we need to be healthy and strong. As a large portion of the global population of all beings, we ingest water and food with little thought or sense of gratitude for the fuel that drives our bodies. Most people in the industrialized world can get water anytime they want by simply turning on their taps. We can bathe and wash our clothes easily in water that seems so abundantly available. Access to water is so common that we take it for granted.

Given the trend of global warming, the abundance of easy access to water is changing. In January 2018, it was expected that Cape Town, South Africa would be the first major city to run out of water within ninety days.[44] Thanks to stringent water restrictions, the city has managed to keep some water flowing but not without restricting water usage to fifty litres/day per person. Our sense of gratitude increases when the thing we are consuming is scarce. However, even when water is abundant where is our feeling of gratitude for this essential element to our survival? When we pollute our oceans, lakes, and rivers, we are polluting ourselves. This can only lead to pain and suffering. Caring for and promoting

---

[43] Time, How a Vegetarian Diet could Help Save the Planet, Justin Worland, March 21, 2016 http://time.com/4266874/vegetarian-diet-climate-change/
[44] Global News, Canada January 16, 2018 https://globalnews.ca/news/3967288/cape-town-running-out-of-water-crisis/

the wise use of scarce resources, like water, contribute to our level of inner serenity. We cannot be at peace within ourselves when we are struggling to find clean drinking water. Our sense of inner calm grows when we acknowledge and are grateful for the nutrients that sustain us. There is a reciprocal appreciation when we care for the earth's water, as we are actually caring for ourselves. When we truly care for ourselves, we take care of all phenomenon.

The consciousness with which we eat also has a bearing on our degree of inner contentment. Being aware of what we eat and being fully present as we consume the fruits, vegetables, meats and grains in our diet will increase our degree of satisfaction and happiness. When we eat our food slowly and with conscious gratitude, we feel greater contentment. Too often in our busy twenty-first-century lives we are rushing to eat or are distracted while eating by our cell phones or televisions. Gratification can only occur when we are present enough to fully enjoy the sights, smells and flavours of our food.

As we eat, we also need to acknowledge the life force that is giving of itself in order for us to survive. The plants are giving of themselves so that we can live another day. It may seem odd to think of plants in this way, but scientists have recently discovered plants have a level of awareness within themselves. In his book *Plant-Thinking: A Philosophy of Vegetal Life* researcher Michael Marder reveals the discovery that plants release to other parts of the plant an airborne biochemical substance when in danger (e.g., from attacking insects).[45] For this to occur,

---

[45] Plant-Thinking: A Philosophy of Vegetal Life, Michael Marder, University of the Basque Country, Bitoria-Gasteiz

there must be some form of consciousness, albeit different from human consciousness, within a living plant. A life force resides within all phenomenon. Thus, when we eat plants, we are consuming life. Acknowledgement and gratitude foster inner contentment and happiness. Our inner peace grows, and we live more in the recognition that all phenomenon is life.

The way in which we raise, treat and butcher animals for consumption is another factor that impacts our inner contentment. As hunter-gatherers, humans killed only what needed for food and were more acknowledging of the life that had been given for our survival. Within some indigenous groups, there is a prayer and sense of gratitude that is offered at the moment of a kill to acknowledge the life that has been taken in order that others may survive.

As humans became less nomadic and embraced farming, animals were raised for the benefit of our families and communities. Our domestic herds had pastures and countryside to roam in as they ate. There they grew and proliferated. Today, so much of our domestic meat is raised in massive buildings in which the animals may be living in crowded and caged conditions, never being able to roam freely. Animals have become a commodity for our consumption. The demand for meat has grown as our global population has exponentially expanded, increasing the need for mass production with accelerated growth times for animals.

Undoubtedly in some cases, animals raised for consumption are treated inhumanely and are either fed or injected with substances to shorten their growth time to meet the unending demand for meat. Most consumers are oblivious to the suffering of the animals they consume as the slaughter is done away from the masses. Merchants display meat in neat, clean packaging in a pleasant and sanitized store. So how does this affect our sense of inner peace? First, we cannot separate ourselves from all phenomenon, and what happens to other life forms has an impact on our own state of consciousness. Furthermore, the fear and trauma the animals experience, either in captivity or as part of the slaughter process, goes into the meat we consume.

Just like the fight or flight response we have in moments of fear or anxiety, animals too experience the adrenaline rush as they are sent for slaughter. The stress hormones go into the animal's blood stream and into the meat we consume. When we eat the meat, we are also energetically eating the trauma experienced by the animal at the moment of death.[46] We are what we eat and our level of inner contentment is negatively affected by the meat we consume. Choosing a vegetarian diet, either occasionally or regularly, promotes a greater sense of peace within our being while contributing to greater peace within the world amongst all beings.

There is growing scientific evidence of the health benefits of eating a vegetarian diet. Some recent evidence suggests that the traditional American food chart should be changed in terms of the proportions of what we eat. The largest portion of our diet should be the consumption of fruit and vegetables, followed by grains, then dairy and then meat as the smallest portion. A lighter diet based primarily on vegetables and fruit shifts our energy. We feel lighter and less heavy physically, mentally, emotionally and energetically.

---

[46] Steady Health, Hormones in Animals and Meat Quality, Delialah Falcon, ND Mar 19, 2012

There is a greater sense of contentment and joy within our being. Some research suggests that a vegetarian diet is:

1. Richer in certain nutrients
2. More conducive to losing weight
3. Helpful in lowering blood sugar and improving kidney function
4. Linked to a lower risk of certain types of cancer
5. Linked to a lower risk of heart disease
6. Helpful in reducing the pain from arthritis[47]

There is also growing research that a vegetarian diet has a positive impact on our planet. The author of an Oxford study, Marco Springmann, suggests that a vegetarian diet would save 7.3 million lives by 2050, reduce greenhouse gas by up to 63% and save $1 trillion annually in reduced healthcare costs and lost productivity.[48] Living in a way that is harmonious and loving toward all living beings and our environment means we are living more harmoniously within ourselves. While a vegetarian diet may not be for everyone, choosing to eat more vegetarian meals and less meat will help our planet and increase our sense of inner peace and harmony.

Our inner contentment is also impacted by the way our food is prepared and how we eat it. When we prepare our

---

[47] Healthline Newsletter, Alina Petre MS, RE (CA) September 23, 2016 https://www.healthline.com/nutrition/vegan-diet-benefits#section2
[48] Time, How a Vegetarian diet could help save the Planet, Justin Worland, March 21, 2016 http://time.com/4266874/vegetarian-diet-climate-change/

food with love and compassion, that is what we consume. Similarly, if we are angry or upset when we are preparing our food, that energy goes into the food and we consume it. Taking the time to be conscious about the way we prepare our food will have a direct impact on our sense of inner harmony. Consider a time when you were upset or angry as you were preparing a meal. Did you enjoy the meal? Was there a sense of contentment and joy in consuming the meal?

The environment in which we prepare the food also has an effect on it energetically. Harsh music or negative news stories are embedded into the foods we eat. Choosing to surround ourselves with harmonious sounds and a healthy environment when you prepare food will create a greater sense of contentment and peace when the food is eaten. Similarly, when we eat our food, doing so in an environment that is peaceful and serene will allow us to take in greater joy and harmony as we eat.

During silent meditation retreats, participants eat in silence so they can be present and enjoy the experience of eating their food. Too often our dining experience is filled with conversation or entertainment that can distract us from the joys of tasting and experiencing our food. Additionally, distractions during eating, such as watching television, mean that we cannot be aware of what we are consuming. We eat quickly, often not even realizing what we have eaten. In many religious traditions, meals begin with a moment of acknowledgement and gratitude for the food and its preparation. For many, we have lost this recognition, and in doing so have lost the sense of peace that comes with appreciation for what we are eating.

In his book *How to Eat* Thich Nhat Hanh writes about taking time to pause and acknowledge the food we have before us. He advises us to take one mouthful and then put down our utensil to fully chew and enjoy our food while eating in silence.[49] There is something very peaceful and nourishing about taking the time to prepare and eat a meal with conscious awareness. We feel greater fulfillment and gratitude for the nourishment that the universe has provided. We experience a sense of harmony within our being and with all phenomenon. Consciously choosing what we eat, how we prepare it and how we eat it has a direct correlation with our inner contentment.

Lastly, it is one thing to take another life for nourishment and survival. It is a far different thing to take a life as a trophy or for a tusk or horn. In these situations, there is a flagrant disregard for the life of another being and the right of all living beings to live in peace and harmony. We cannot expect to live in harmony and peace within ourselves when we are not loving and compassionate toward all living beings. I can think of no justification for such actions other than for dominance over another being or for some misguided belief of a perceived health benefit. In these situations, we all have an opportunity to look deeply within ourselves to explore why we feel warranted in taking this action and why we as human beings allow such actions to take place. When we are honouring of all life (e.g., an elephant, a rhino, an insect, etc.) we begin to develop our own sense of honouring of the life within us. By caring for all living beings, we are caring for ourselves. The degree to which we experience inner peace is a reflection of the peace and harmony we put out into the world.

---

[49] How to Eat, Thich Nhat Hanh, Parallax Press

Practical application

To apply what you have learned in this section, try one or two of the suggestions below. Take a step, test the water or jump in with both feet. The choice is yours.

Take a step:

- Take a moment to give thanks for the food you are about to eat. This practice is a part of many traditions around the world, including indigenous peoples, Christians, Buddhists, Muslims and Jews.

- Prepare meals in an environment that is positive and loving.

Test the water:

- Eat your evening meals in silence for one week. Pause after every spoonful to enjoy the flavours fully before taking another bite.

- Look for ways to use less water: take shorter showers, flush the toilet only when necessary, use xeriscape landscaping techniques in your yard.

Jump in with both feet:

- Eat more vegetarian meals.

- Buy locally raised meat from farmers whose cattle are allowed to graze outdoors.

- Support fundraising efforts to clean up our waterways and oceans.

Sense impressions

> *This being human is a guest house.*
> *Every morning a new arrival.*
> *A joy, a depression, a meanness, some momentary awareness comes as an unexpected visitor.*
> *Welcome and entertain them all!*
> *~ Jalal Ad-Din Mohammed Rumi*

Food is just one form of nourishment that we consume. Everything we see and hear flows into our consciousness and impacts and shapes our thoughts, feelings and perspectives. The material we read, the entertainment we watch and the games we play are all integrated into our psyche, influencing our inner peace and affecting how we see the world. Consciously choosing, with awareness, what we take in through our eyes either increases or decreases our inner contentment. The sounds we hear also impact our inner peace in equally important ways. All forms of sound, such as radio, tv, music, electronic games, and conversations affect our consciousness and play a role in determining our inner tranquility. Just as we are selective with the food we eat, we too must be discerning about the visual and auditory stimulation we allow into our being. It is through conscious discernment of all we consume that we foster inner contentment.

We are bombarded with visual stimulation from the moment we open our eyes. All of the sights around us influence our thinking and our view of the world. The experience we have when we open our eyes to a sunny beach with rolling ocean waves is very different from opening our eyes to watch the global turmoil on the news. Each view is taken in through our senses and is processed within our consciousness, shaping our perceptions. We are either consciously or unconsciously programming our perceptions of the world, based on what we see. Reading about or seeing violent acts disturbs our inner contentment, and we become inwardly agitated by what we see. When we continually read or watch the news, we may be inundated with negative, distressing thoughts and feelings. Movies and television series become a reality, if only for a moment, and we begin to believe what we see is real.

Many people, and in particular children, play electronic video games for hours at a time. Often the most popular video games are those that are about violence.[50] This violence is imbedded into the consciousness of the players who can become desensitized[51] to these actions. While there is ongoing debate as to whether this desensitization leads to external acts of violence,[52] we know that whatever we put our focus on grows. Similarly, some watch the daily news as though it is a reality television show. We see others experiencing tragedy and trauma; yet, we are detached

---

[50] Huff Post Contributor Platform, Common Sense Media Contributor, June 24, 3013 https://www.huffingtonpost.com/common-sense-media/10-most-violent-video-games_b_3480497.html

[51] Psychology Today, Violent Video Games can Trigger Emotional Desensitization, Christopher Bergland, April 9, 2016 https://www.psychologytoday.com/us/blog/the-athletes-way/201604/violent-video-games-can-trigger-emotional-desensitization

[52] verywellFamily, Do Violent Video Games Really Lead to Aggressive Behavior?, Amy Morin LCSW, January 18, 2109 https://www.verywellfamily.com/aggressive-behavior-and-video-games-1094980

CBS News, Do violent video games lead to criminal behaviour? Michael Casey, Aug 17, 2015 https://www.cbsnews.com/news/do-violent-video-games-lead-to-criminal-behavior/

from the pain of their experience. In some ways, we become numb to the global turmoil.

When we consciously choose what we take in through our eyes, we can be selective of those things that promote inner harmony. Choosing non-violent video games, reading books about compassion and kindness or deciding to reduce our time watching the nightly news are ways in which we can be cognizant of what we are consuming through our eyes. It is challenging for us to be peaceful and compassionate toward others when we are not fostering these attributes within ourselves. Being aware of what we are consuming through our visual stimuli has a direct bearing on our inner contentment.

In the same way, the things we hear also shape our consciousness and perspective of the world. The music we listen to, the radio, the television, the conversations and the other sounds in our environment all influence how we see the world. Consider the music you listen to on a regular basis. Are the words loving and kind or negative and depressing? A great deal of music, across most genres, is about either wanting or losing a beloved in a love relationship. We listen to our favorite music repeatedly, engraving the words into our consciousness. In many ways, we are programming our minds with the repetitive words we listen to.

Choosing music that is uplifting and has a positive message adds to our inner contentment. Similarly, the words we hear while listening to the radio or watching television are also interwoven into our psyche. Choosing to listen to entertainment that is inspiring and positive increases our happiness and joy. Far too often, we neglect to think about what we are feeding our minds throughout the day. In so many cases, our entertainment is a distraction from our own consciousness and is a way to escape from having to listen to ourselves and be present in the moment.

A significant portion of our auditory listening is in the conversations we have with other people throughout our day. Conversations with family members, colleagues and people we happen to interact with also influence our thinking and perceptions of the world. For many of us, our key relationships are with family members. The conversations with our spouse, children, parents or extended family can weigh heavily on how we see the world. When the dialogue is loving and kind, we feel positive and upbeat. We may even feel supported and cared for, which nurtures our sense of inner contentment.

In contrast, when our conversations are negative and unloving, we can feel disharmony and frustration within ourselves. Given that these are typically the most significant relationships in our lives, it may be difficult to simply extract oneself from the conversation. When these types of discussions are repeated, we are engraining them into our being. We are allowing our consciousness to be won over by the disharmonious dialogue in our life.

Similarly, conversations with work colleagues or friends can have an equal impact on our sense of inner peace. It is challenging to walk away from a boss who is disrespectful or overly critical. Having to work with someone who may be angry or unhappy weighs on our own inner peace. In some cases, we are not even aware of the impact conversations are having on our happiness.

Actively listening to a conversation that is unfolding and considering whether or not it is adding to or distracting from our feeling of inner peace helps us decide when to be engaged and when to extract ourselves. Being aware of and contemplating the types of exchanges we want to have with people can build on our inner harmony.

One final consideration is the role we play in adding to conversations. Are we loving and kind in our responses to other people? When we interact with others, are we able to come from a place of peace and tranquility, or are we simply adding fuel to the fire? When we communicate from a place of peace and calm, we influence the conversation with our presence. Fostering a state of contentment allows us to be open and curious in our interactions with others. Through our presence, we also create the space for others to be receptive and relaxed. The world we experience is based on the lens we choose to view it through. When we choose to come from a perspective of harmony and contentment, our world reflects this peaceful viewpoint.

I am not suggesting we should exclude ourselves from life by turning off the television, not going to movies, or avoiding family, friends and colleagues. Nor should we only allow happy situations into our life. That would be unrealistic. Rather, the perspective being presented here is that we must choose what we allow to flow into our consciousness. It is important to be consciously aware of what we allow into our being and to challenge our perspectives of life and the world. As the quote by Rumi at the beginning of this section says, "Welcome and entertain them all." We must welcome what surfaces in our lives while pondering whether it is true and how it serves us in creating greater happiness and peace.

This dance of dynamic peace is the undulation of active engagement in life while remaining focused on creating inner peace. Wade Boggs, a twentieth century American baseball player said, "Our lives are not determined by what happens to us but how we react to what happens, not by what life brings us but the attitude we bring to life." When we are centered within ourselves in a place of inner harmony, we are more open and receptive to life. We see what life brings us with greater clarity and from a broader point of view. Nurturing a state of dynamic inner peace allows us to be more present to what life offers. We are able to receive openly and to make conscious choices about how we respond to life.

The environment in which we live also adds to our sense of inner serenity. The place in which we choose to live and work influences the joy and happiness we experience. We get a different feeling being in a big city than out in nature. The city is filled with many diverse people, busy streets and tall buildings. There is an energy of hustle and bustle in the city as people go about their daily lives. Many people experience a sense of anonymity amongst the large population as they go about their errands. The sights and sounds can be over stimulating for some, while others have developed the ability to be immune to the barrage of stimuli. In the city, there are so many minds thinking that the collective conscious energy is active and disharmonious. A greater effort is required to remain true to oneself and not get caught up in the distractions of city life.

In comparison, the experience of being out in nature can be recharging and calming. The rustle of the wind in the trees, the chirping of the birds, the sight of a deer or the panoramic view of a mountain range fill our being with peace and serenity. We breath easier and our mind becomes more still. Our soul is rejuvenated with prana (lifeforce) and life becomes clearer. We need to spend time in the environment that fosters inner peace and recharges our being. Noticing which environments serve us and which deplete us helps us create greater inner harmony and contentment.

Practical application

To apply what you have learned in this section, try one or two of the suggestions below. Take a step, test the water or jump in with both feet. The choice is yours.

Take a step:

- Regularly go for walks in the park or in nature.

- Consider ways to create greater harmony in your home. Pick one thing to implement. For example: light a scented candle, have a regular quiet time during the day, create a quiet space in your home.

Test the water:

- Choose to watch TV shows and movies that are non-violent and life affirming.

- Reduce the time your children play violent video games.

Jump in with both feet:

- Watch the news only once per day, week or month.

- Promote loving and kind conversations in your home and work environment. Ensure that everyone speaks in a loving and compassionate way toward others in your home.

Volition

> *No desires, no goal, no seeking, no thoughts,*
> *neither obtaining, nor rejecting, nor grasping,*
> *nor letting go, being free.*
> *~ Taisen Deshimaru*

The principle of cause and effect suggests that for every action there will be a corresponding reaction. Through our free will (our volition), we take action that results in a subsequent reaction. According to the Merriam-Webster dictionary, volition is "the act or power of making one's own choices or decisions." Action is always in a direction as a result of making a choice or decision, including the choice to do nothing. Yet, when our will causes us to act, do our actions align with our greatest good? Does our will to act arise out of an intention to be loving, kind and compassionate? Regardless of our intentions, we always experience the product of our action. Our deeds either nourish us or deplete us. In making conscious choices with awareness, our conduct will be inspired by our highest good. Thus, our volition has the ability to nurture or dampen our inner peace and contentment.

Our actions arise out of our thoughts, desires and intentions. All actions move us either towards or away from inner peace. This is the constant shifting and changing dance of dynamic peace. At times, we are quite conscious of the choices we are making and our will to act is deliberate and focused, such as deciding which route to take to work. We may listen to the traffic radio station to know where the road congestion is and then select the best route for our commute. In this case, we are consciously thinking about traffic, time and urgency, which then influence us to act in a way that addresses these concerns. As a result, we arrive at work on time and in a peaceful state.

At other times, our strong desires can cause us to act without being clear about our intentions. We may find we are powerfully attracted to someone and act in a way that we would not typically act. Our deep desire sways us to take action which may or may not create a favourable outcome. It is in these moments we get glimpses into our underlying desires and may even be surprised by our experience. There may be times we believe we are acting out of our true intentions and yet feel baffled by the result of our actions. Somehow the situation creates a disconnect from our belief about our desired or intended outcome. These moments awaken us to create a stronger alignment between our thoughts and actions, which then fosters inner peace.

I can recall a time when I reacted angrily towards a family member over an unexpected change in travel plans. My reaction created anger and distance in our relationship. Upon reflection, I realized my reaction was rooted in feeling hurt and unappreciated. Later we spoke, and I was better able to articulate my true feelings, leading to a more honest and harmonious outcome. If we approach a situation from a place of peace and compassion, we create and generate peace and compassion. If we approach a situation from a place of anger and frustration, we proliferate anger and frustration.

Regardless of whether our will or intention to act is clear, we will always be impacted by the outcome of our actions. When our actions are based on ego gratification, that is what we experience. Consider the madness of people climbing over one another to get the best Boxing Day or Black Friday deals. The frenzied rush consumes the shoppers and all sense of right action disappears. When we act with loving kindness and compassion, our actions engender a corresponding reaction. An example of this is caring for a lost and injured animal or having compassion for our fellow humans who may be suffering as a result of a tragedy. Choosing to use our will to act from a place of peaceful, conscious awareness promotes peace in our lives and in the world.

Our volition can increase or decrease our sense of inner contentment. When our actions are in alignment with our intention, we feel in harmony with ourselves. Yet, when our actions create an unexpected response, we can feel confused and even perplexed. Perhaps there was a time when you gave a surprise birthday party for a friend only to find your friend was not happy about it. Maybe you performed an act of kindness for a family member but they felt you had interfered in their life. It could be that you worked long and hard on a project at work only to find your boss unhappy with your efforts. The disconnect we feel arising out of our actions shows us our innermost expectations and goals.

When we feel a disconnect, it is a perfect opportunity to look at our expectations behind our actions. Perhaps our good intentions were coming from a place of self-gratification. In this case, our inner peace may be disturbed by the corresponding outcome of our actions. Yet, our perspective determines whether we interpret the outcome as positive or negative. Alternatively, we can take the view that everything that arises provides greater insight into discovering our true nature and reinforces the perspective that life is a continuous ever-changing and dynamic unfolding of insight into ourselves. Whatever surfaces is an opportunity to be self-reflective, with curiosity and intrigue. From this point of view, as we learn to welcome whatever surfaces, with curiosity and openness, our inner peace grows.

When our volition is made with conscious awareness rising out of loving compassion and kindness, we foster greater bliss in our lives and the lives of those around us. We can rest in contentment when our actions originate from our highest intentions and come from the perspective of not causing harm (ahimsa). For example, when we feel anger swelling up inside us, we can choose not to act but to look inward to see what is going on underneath our anger. Once we have looked into our anger, we can then express our true feelings with kindness and a perspective of seeking to understand the underlying belief(s) that have brought up our anger.

We have seen this possibility in the forgiveness by a victim's family members who choose to speak with kindness toward the perpetrator. Their will to act has come from a place of inner reflection to see not only their suffering but also the anguish of the person who has caused harm. Whatever the resulting outcome, we can be at peace within ourselves knowing we have acted from a compassionate viewpoint of kind-heartedness and humanitarianism. From this place, we are able to honour all living beings and be accepting of the choices they make in their lives. When our free will to act comes from a place of inner peace, our actions will always be peaceful.

Practical application

To apply what you have learned in this section, try one or two of the suggestions below. Take a step, test the water or jump in with both feet. The choice is yours.

Take a step:

- Reflect on a recent decision and its resulting outcome. Did your actions align with your intent and have the desired result?

- Consider how can you could be kinder and more compassionate yet still achieve your desired goals?

Test the water:

- Think about an action you took that did not have the desired results. What was your true intention? What action will you take moving forward?

- Reflect on an action you have taken that caused harm to another being. What did you learn? What will you do differently next time? Is there a way to remedy your harmful actions? If so, take action.

Jump in with both feet:

- When feeling angry, first pause to reflect on your anger to understand its origins. Then speak with kindness to the other person who brought out this anger in you.

- Take action toward someone out of pure kindness and compassion without expectation of reward or benefit. Notice the impact this action has on the receiver and on yourself.

Consciousness

> *Do not look for sanctuary in anyone except yourself.*
> *~ Buddha*

Every thought we have ever had has brought us to this present moment. Our thoughts have shaped the person we have become and are the genesis of our beliefs and perspectives. Thoughts are like the seeds we plant in our garden of consciousness.[53] We need to attend to our garden, nurturing the thoughts we want and pulling out the rest like weeds. As with any garden, what we water and nurture grows, so being conscious of the thoughts we want to cultivate determines our future.

Growing and maintaining inner peace means we need to foster those thoughts that create peace and harmony within our being. At the same time, there is a collective consciousness that we both contribute to and are a part of. Our collective consciousness is the culmination of a number of shared beliefs arising out of our family life, community, culture and the larger global society. In some cases, our collective consciousness helps us to evolve peacefully, while at other times, we may need to transform our collective consciousness in order to advance peace.

Many quantum mechanics scientists have come to the conclusion that reality does not exist without an observer

---

[53] An Exploration of Mindfulness in Education: Mindfulness Retreat for Educators, Thich Nhat Hanh, Brock University, Ontario Canada Aug 11-16, 2013

to observe it.[54]. In other words, the physical reality cannot exist without subjectivity. This premise is known as the Copenhagen Interpretation. Without consciousness, there is no physical matter.[55] It would appear that science is catching up with the teachings of the mystics who have known for centuries we create reality through our thoughts. What we think, feel, perceive and believe is real. Through conscious awareness we are creating reality in each moment.

To live a life that is harmonious and full of contentment, we must take full ownership of our thoughts. From the moment of our birth, every thought that has surfaced has shaped us into the person we are today. Our thoughts about our parents, family, environment, culture, community, the earth and the cosmos have interwoven into the mosaic of our beliefs, views and perspectives about ourselves and the world. We use our senses to interact with the world, sparking thoughts that lead to feelings about the environment around us and ourselves.

From our thoughts and feelings, we create beliefs and perspectives that help us navigate our internal and external worlds. These beliefs we hold to be true, together with the perspectives we maintain about ourselves and the world, are the framework of our identification with ourselves. If we change a belief, we change our view of ourselves and of

---

[54] HackSpirit, Reality is an illusion: The scientific proof everything is energy and reality isn't real, Lachlan Brown, January 19, 2018 https://hackspirit.com/illusion-reality-scientific-proof-everything-energy-reality-isnt-real/
[55] The Healers Journal, Quantum Physics Explains How Your Thoughts Create Reality, January 9, 2014 https://www.thehealersjournal.com/2014/01/09/quantum-physics-thoughts/

life. A very simple illustration of this phenomenon can be drawn from the ancient notion that the world is flat. We now know the earth is indeed a sphere and that sailing off in one direction can ultimately lead you back to the same place from which you started. By changing the long-held belief that the world is flat, our collective consciousness shifted to view the world in a completely different way. Similarly, consider a time when you believed a situation or person was a certain way only to find out you were wrong. Perhaps, while vacationing in another country, you discovered the view you had of the people and culture there was quite different from reality. Maybe the person you had been in a relationship with was not the person you believed him/her to be. When we change our perspective, we change how we view the world and how we interact in and with that world.

The thoughts we nurture and attend to create our garden of consciousness. Whatever thought we care for and water continues to grow. When we support thoughts of anger, frustration, hatred and aggression they grow and flourish within our consciousness. Living without awareness of the thoughts we are cultivating, can leave us living a life that is unfulfilling and disappointing.

Just as our previous thoughts have brought us to this moment in time, our continued thinking creates our future. When our perspective is that life should be different, we can see the effect our accumulated thoughts and feelings that have brought us to this moment of dissatisfaction. In this very moment, we can look into our life for areas of unhappiness. What are the thoughts and feelings we are harbouring that are contributing to our discontent? Our ingrained belief that life should be a certain way bumps up against how life actually is in each moment. A simple, yet profound quote to this effect was offered by Ajahn Chah, a Thai Buddhist monk, who said, "This is the way it is." We may believe we have worked hard and deserve better or that we are entitled to life being a certain way. Yet, what is real is this very moment. The belief or perspective we hold about it is simply that: a belief. Change our belief and the world will look very different.

To live with greater inner peace and happiness, we must nurture thoughts that are peaceful and harmonious. By increasing our awareness of our thoughts and consciously deciding which ones we will nurture and which ones we will let die, we can increase our level of joy and contentment. Through conscious awareness, we begin to really see our thoughts and explore the underlying beliefs that create them. As we begin to see our unhappiness arises from within, we can consciously make choices that foster happiness in each and every moment.

In my own life, there have been times when I have continually watered negative thinking, which lead to periods of personal suffering. At the age of fifty-four, I was diagnosed with prostate cancer. My negative thoughts of worry and anxiety began to dominate my thinking. I was clearly watering the seeds of my own suffering. My constant worry did not change the outcome, but it greatly increased my level of suffering. It only when we catch our recurring negative thinking and consciously decide not to nurture it, that we are able to foster more positive thoughts and alleviate our suffering.

When inner conflict surfaces, turning towards it and looking at the thoughts and perspectives that are reinforcing our struggle will help us release our limiting views. Inner peace and contentment will always be a dynamic process of discovery and illumination. When we have the courage to be present with ourselves and look underneath our thoughts, we soon find the wherewithal to be with what is, allowing peace to unfold within us. If we can catch and challenge our thinking before it becomes an integrated belief or perspective, we go a long way to living a more peaceful and joyous life, moment to moment.

As human beings, we are also part of a collective consciousness with other beings. Our families, culture, communities and larger society shape our thinking. From the moment of our birth, our parents, siblings and extended family influence how we think, act and behave. Our view of the external world, and what we think of ourselves and other people is affected by the thoughts shared within our family. The words our parents use to describe situations, events and other people become embedded into our consciousness and begin to inform our beliefs about the world. We naturally align our thinking with the thinking of those around us so we fit in and become part of the collective.

There is an affinity that is formed with our family and close friends. When we encounter people who are different from us, we look toward those closest to us to determine how we should interact and respond. These views can be further reinforced through our cultural associations. We have seen extreme times around the world when our cultural consciousness has led to atrocities and injustice. The genocides that occurred during World War II, the Bosnian war and more recently the war in Syria are examples of culturally based consciousness causing much pain and suffering. In many cases, it is hard to undo the engrained beliefs and views of our families and culture.

We also identify with our larger communities and country. There is pride and nationalism in being Canadian, American, South African, Japanese, etc. Our consciousness is shaped by our nationalistic perspectives influencing how we behave and act in the world. Olympics, World Cups or national sporting events create immense pride and patriotism within our consciousness. These deeply held cultural and nationalistic views influence our thinking on a large scale and can be challenging to change.

Yet, we also have the ability to be an influencer of the collective consciousness that we are a part of. Our own thinking, views and perspectives can influence those around us. Whether we know it or not, we have great influence on others and can play a role in creating greater harmony and peace amongst family members, cultures, communities and the global consciousness. There are many examples of people who have greatly influenced our larger consciousness and brought about global change. Martin Luther King Jr., Nelson Mandela, Rosa Parks, Mahatma Gandhi, and Susan B. Anthony each inspired cultural change on a larger scale. When we live a life based on nurturing inner peace and harmony, we become a beacon of calm and tranquility that others are drawn to, like a hummingbird to a flower.

We have the ability to encourage inner peace and serenity in others and that can have an exponential impact on the collective consciousness. Challenging our own biases and limiting beliefs with compassion and kindness alters our consciousness and sends subtle waves of change into the collective. Creating a life that is fulfilling and aligned with our core values shows others a way to live that is more harmonious and gratifying. Being aware of and owning our thoughts enables us to live in harmony within ourselves as the never-ending ups and downs of life unfold. Our outer world begins to reflect the calm of our inner world, while we simultaneously foster overall peace.

We must also take ownership and accountability for our own thoughts and the world we are creating for ourselves as a result of our thinking. While our mind may think non-stop, we must still take ownership of the thoughts we nurture and discard. This ability begins when we become consciously aware of our thoughts.

Seldom are we aware of our thoughts as they surface. Most of us are caught up in our own worlds and thoughts throughout the day. There are times when we let our minds run on autopilot, creating stories, conversations and solving problems in our heads. Perhaps we cannot remember how we drove home, but we know we solved an issue at work. It may appear our thoughts are in fact consciousness, but then who is it that is observing our thoughts? There is witness consciousness that observes our thoughts and actions. It is ever present and wakeful whenever we stop to notice. From this viewpoint, we see our thoughts for what they are, simply the data processing of all the external stimuli interfacing with our feelings and beliefs to create some semblance of order. Yet, these thoughts are our own and as such we must own them and be accountable for what arises from them.

Most people have the mistaken notion that we should believe everything our mind tells us. The mind's role is to think, which it does extremely well. However, not all thoughts are worth saving or investing more time in. Ownership and accountability mean that we see our thoughts and decide which ones serve our highest good and which ones need to be discarded. We must be accountable to weed out the thoughts that are violent, harmful and self-negating. Experience and conditioning have shown us not to take action on all of our thoughts. As children we learn not to hit and as adults we learned to take responsibility for our actions.

To create greater peace and harmony in our lives we must learn to nourish thoughts of peace and kindness and to discourage racist and hateful thinking. We must learn to be the alert, attentive witness to our thoughts, to consciously decide which ones to cultivate and then to take mindful action to create a peaceful and joyous future. Meditation is the practical tool that enables us to see and take ownership of our thoughts. And it is in the quiet witnessing of our thoughts, that peace and compassion flourish.

Practical application

To apply what you have learned in this section, try one or two of the suggestions below. Take a step, test the water or jump in with both feet. The choice is yours.

Take a step:

- Begin to notice which thoughts you are nurturing within your own garden of consciousness. Which thoughts will you continue to grow and which will you pull out?

- Look at different cultures to see how their beliefs differ from your own. What insights did you gain about your own cultural perspectives as a result?

Test the water:

- Recognize that it is your own thoughts, feelings and beliefs about the world that create your happiness or suffering. Consciously choose thoughts that foster joy and contentment.

- Notice negative or harmful thoughts and consciously decide to make changes to release them. Write out your negative thoughts and then ceremonially burn the paper, make an agreement within yourself to catch and remove negative thoughts, or think or say a positive statement to replace a harmful thought.

Jump in with both feet:

- Journal daily and re-write ideas/thoughts that you want to change in order to live a more peaceful life.

- Take ownership for areas of unhappiness in your life and actively make changes to live with greater joy.

Chapter Five: Exploring Self

*Five enemies of peace inhabit with us:
avarice, ambition, envy, anger, and pride.
If these were to be banished, we should
infallibly enjoy perpetual peace.*
~ Francesco Petrarca

Judgemental mind

> *To know others is to have wisdom.*
> *To know oneself is to gain enlightenment.*
> *~ Lao-Tzu*

From an early age, we are conditioned to evaluate and judge events, situations and people as being positive or negative, good or bad. We are drawn toward those things that we like and repulsed by those things we do not. Over the years, we develop beliefs about how situations and people should be, and we form opinions about what is right and wrong. Not surprisingly, some of our most intense judgements can be about ourselves. We critique and criticize our own physical appearance, mental aptitude or emotional strength. Our internal self-dialogue may be overly harsh and disparaging. Self-denigration always pulls us away from experiencing inner peace and joy.

Through years of conditioning, some of our thoughts become so automatic, we do not even notice them or realize their impact on us. These thoughts run though our minds unchallenged, reinforcing negative thinking. Based on our own view of the world, we also pass judgements about other people, such as how they should be or how they should have responded. Being aware of our judgemental thoughts and courageously looking beneath them to see the truth behind our beliefs, frees us from viewing the world through a distorted perspective and creates space for greater inner peace and contentment.

Throughout our life, we become accustomed to evaluating and assessing situations, events and even people. At an early age, children are open and accepting of others and situations because they have not yet been conditioned to judge. They easily make friends with other children of different gender, race, ethnicity and religion. Children have little concern for skin colour or cultural customs. They just want to play with other children. Yet, our children so easily pick up on the judgements and biases of their parents and other adults around them. They soon learn to place judgements on other children, saying things like "Mary comes from another country and my dad doesn't like her family, so I won't play with her" or "Adam's family goes to a different church and my parents don't want me playing with him." Unfortunately, early childhood judgements are often carried forward into adulthood. We become conditioned to judge other people by their appearance, actions and place of origin. In the same way, we learn to form opinions about the things that other people do, such as "Johnny likes to play with dolls but boys shouldn't do that" or "Juanita wants to play hockey but that's only for boys."

As we grow, we learn to associate with others who have similar views and perspectives. We want to fit in so we align ourselves with others who have similar points of view. Perhaps you liked sports growing up so you made friends with others who played sports. Maybe you liked to read and study so you allied yourself with other voracious readers. As a result of our associations, we exclude people from other groups, becoming strangers to their views and perspectives of the world. Those we do not associate with become outsiders, and in some cases, people we fear. Our view of the world is restricted by what we allow into our inner circle. As a result, we often create uninformed opinions about situations and people based on our limited internal perspective.

A judgemental mind takes us away from experiencing the moment. In this way, we are the first ones to suffer as a result of our own judgements. The negative impact of our judgemental thoughts affects us before having any consequences for anyone else. This truth was spoken about over 2,500 years ago by the Buddha who said, "Do not be the judge of people; do not make assumptions about others. A person is destroyed by holding judgments about others." Our judgements take us further away from inner peace and harmony. Awareness of our judgemental thoughts enables us to look behind our beliefs and awaken to our deepest truths. Only by turning toward ourselves and candidly looking at our own judgemental mind can we find inner peace.

Some of our harshest judgements are the thoughts and beliefs we hold about ourselves. Most people have critical thoughts about their physical appearance. If we listen to our inner dialogue, we often hear language about being too short, tall, fat or thin. Each time we look in the mirror, we may see features we dislike. Our ears or nose are too big. Our eyes are too small or are the wrong colour. Our hair won't style right or is prematurely turning grey.

Perhaps others have made hurtful comments about our appearance and we have come to believe them, thus altering our own perspective of ourselves. In the Western world of the twenty-first century, masculine men are portrayed as strong, fit and emotionally stoic. As a young man, I was very thin with lean muscle mass. At times, I felt inadequate simply because of my non-muscular physique. My internal dialogue was judgemental and overly self-critical. It was not until I learned to love and accept myself as I am, that I was able to release my negative self-image.

The most beautiful women in the Western world are pictured as tall, with slender shapely bodies. Yet, even super models, who tend to be young, tall and slender, are often judged for being too heavy or not having the right eyes or face shape to be selected for a modeling job. The image we hold about how we should look creates judgemental thoughts about how we are. We are unaccepting of ourselves because we believe we should look a certain way to fit into societal norms. The judgemental thoughts we have about ourselves prevent us from feeling love and acceptance for ourselves. Repetitive negative thinking inhibits our ability to experience deep contentment. Only through self-acceptance and self-love are we able to settle into the experience of inner peace.

Another area of self-judgement occurs in our thoughts about not being good enough. Whether it is at school, work or in our personal lives we can harbour negative thinking that we are in some way not measuring up. Regardless of whether we believe we are not measuring up to someone else's expectations, it is our expectations of ourselves that result in self-judgement.

For some individuals, who are high-achievers, they often feel driven to push harder, achieve more and keep striving to ever increasing expectations of themselves. They tend to be highly self-critical and their drive to achieve can often be compelled by an inner belief that whatever they do is not good enough. Like all of us, they are looking to find happiness and joy but are never satisfied with what they do. This can often be the case in workplace situations. Comments from our boss or work colleagues can undermine our confidence, leading to self-judgement and criticism. Self-denigration creates a downward spiral of destructive thinking. The degree of internal condemnation can be so great that we are unable to face ourselves, and we lash out at other people in anger.

It is challenging to love and accept ourselves from a place of negativity. Inner harmony and contentment seem unattainable when we are being harsh with ourselves. Courageously turning toward our self-judgement, looking at what is really going on underneath and asking ourselves, "Is it true?" begins the journey of climbing out of this downward spiral. Being watchful of our inner dialogue and choosing language that is loving and supportive, lifts the dark cloud of self-criticism. Through the practice of meditation, we are able to be the non-judgemental witness to our thoughts on a more consistent basis. We see our judgements as they surface and challenge their validity. From a place of self-acceptance and compassion, we are better able to rest our minds on contentment and inner harmony.

Over time, our negative thinking can be so repetitive it becomes automatic. The thoughts have become so engrained into our consciousness that we do not see them or question their validity. For instance, when we continually tell ourselves we are overweight, we believe it is true. Our perspective of ourselves becomes solid and impenetrable. If someone tells us otherwise, we do not believe them, we think they are making a joke of us.

It is challenging to notice the automatic thoughts running through our minds, as they have become a familiar soundtrack on auto play. Yet, we cannot be at peace within ourselves unless we are able to remove the limiting beliefs we hold about ourselves. Only through attentive self-observation and mindfulness can we hope to alter our automatic negative thinking. When we hear ourselves say,

"I am not good enough" or "I don't deserve to," we need to pause and look at the underlying assumption we hold as true about ourselves.

Awareness is always the first step in making a change. Once we are aware of our limiting belief, we can then begin to create more truthful language that is non-judgemental. Through the process of self-awareness, we are able to be more accepting of ourselves moment to moment. Our judgements more easily fall away, and we feel a greater sense of peace and joy within.

Our judgemental mind is not restricted to negative thoughts about ourselves but toward other people as well. We can be quick to pass judgement on others. Perhaps they are not living up to our expectations, or they have done something that does not align with our belief system. Maybe they have said something that has hurt our feelings and we make a quick judgement about their character. We may hear ourselves saying things like "Anthony is so self-centered that he only cares about himself" or "Adelaide is a terrible people leader." Often our judgements are made behind the other person's back. Furthermore, we often actively seek out friends or family who will validate and justify our feelings. At times, we even enroll others into supporting our judgement of others so we are not alone in our belief.

It seems easy and convenient to pass judgement on other people. The blame gets placed on someone else and in someway we do not feel quite so bad. However, the judgemental feelings are ours to own. When we judge others, we are projecting our belief or view of the world onto the other person. They have acted in a way that does not align with our values and therefore they are wrong. We seldom turn toward our judgemental thoughts of others to see our own limiting perspective. Nor do we take the time to try to understand the situation from the other person's point of view. In doing so, we cause ourselves to suffer first and foremost as a result of our judgemental mind.

The Buddha said, "Holding onto anger (judgement) is like grasping a hot coal with the intent of throwing it at someone else; you are the one who gets burned."[56] Being aware and catching ourselves when we have judgemental thoughts of other people provides us with the opportunity to challenge our own beliefs and views. We see that our judgements only truly hurt ourselves, as we try to carry and maintain our critical point of view. When we judge other people, we are taking away from our experience of inner peace and joy.

Practical application

To apply what you have learned in this section, try one or two of the suggestions below. Take a step, test the water or jump in with both feet. The choice is yours.

Take a step:

- What is one judgement you have about someone (e.g., a work colleague or an acquaintance)? Is your perspective true or just something you believe?

- What judgements do you have about yourself (e.g., height, weight, appearance, abilities)? What's one thing you would like to be more accepting of about

---

[56] Brainy Quote, Buddha Quotes https://www.brainyquote.com/quotes/buddha_104025

yourself? Consider how you can be more accepting our yourself.

Test the water:

- Notice how you are the first person to suffer when you hold judgemental thoughts about someone else. Let go of your criticism in order to feel more inner peace.

- Pay attention to automatic critical thinking. Catch yourself and challenge long-held beliefs that prevent you from feeling content.

Jump in with both feet:

- Recognize that someone else's opinion of you is simply that: an opinion. Ask yourself if their criticism is true. If not, let it go and don't hold on to the suffering. If you believe there is validity in what they are saying, what do you need to learn in order to love and accept yourself as you are?

- Notice times when you are seeking others' validation of your judgements or colluding with others to perpetuate criticism of someone else. Stop the cycle of group judgements and look inwardly to see your own judgements of yourself.

Desire

> *There is no greater crime*
> *than not being able to control your desires.*
> *~ Lao-Tzu*

In so many ways, we let our desires consume our thoughts and feelings, and ultimately our actions. These strong forces within our being intensify if they remain unconscious and unchallenged. We long for something or someone to fill a perceived emptiness we believe can only be satisfied through the acquisition of that which we feel is missing. Food, materiality, sexual desire and the need for companionship can dominate our thoughts, creating strong feelings of yearning. Yet, all too often, acquiring the thing that we desire is less satisfying than our belief that we will somehow be fulfilled. We may experience a moment of gratification but eventually that which we desired becomes commonplace, and we once again find ourselves looking to fill a void.

By turning toward our desires and looking at them with conscious awareness, we can address our underlying longing. From there, we can develop greater self-compassion, kindness and contentment as we observe and accept ourselves as we are. Our inner peace reveals itself as we attend to that which is hidden within our desires.

Desire arises out of a perceived emptiness or absence of something or someone whose acquisition, we believe, will bring us greater happiness. We long for that which we believe we do not have in order to feel content. If we only had that new job, new car or new relationship our life would be so much better and we would be happy. Our recurring thoughts that we are somehow lacking evoke strong emotions of desire. When we let these thoughts and feelings go unchallenged, we allow them to grow and strengthen within our being. Essentially, we are watering the seeds of our own discontent. In some cases, our thoughts become obsessive and dominate our consciousness and possibly even our actions. Maybe we long for social acceptance, so we change our appearance, behaviour or friends in order to fit in.

We continually look for gratification in external things or people to fill the void we are feeling within ourselves. Our belief is that we can only get what we need from outside of us. In truth, everything we need in any moment is present and available from within when we stop to notice. Those things that bring us the greatest joy in life are always found within. At the same time, we seldom look at the root cause of our desire to see what is driving us. Our desire for social acceptance may have its roots in a lack of self-acceptance. We are unable to love ourselves as we are, so we seek validation from others in order to feel love. In some cases, it can be hard to get to the root of our desire if we have nurtured them into tall trees in our garden of consciousness. The roots of our desire run deep and are intertwined with other beliefs, making it difficult to see what is at the core. When our desires surface, we must turn our gaze inward, exploring with conscious awareness the origins of our yearnings. Inner peace and contentment cannot be filled by external factors. Unquestioned desire takes us away from experiencing peace and joy and can only lead to greater suffering.

One of our greatest desires is the need for companionship. Humans are social creatures who both need and long for the company of others. Research has consistently shown that we need human connection to grow and survive. Our children must have regular and consistent human contact in order to develop and gain self-recognition.[57] For most humans, our spirit diminishes if we do not have connection with other beings. As we mature, this desire for human companionship becomes focused on finding that special someone to love. So many of our stories, songs and poetry speak to the acquisition and loss of love. On a primal basis, this desire fulfills a purpose of proliferating our species. Yet, it is also about the desire to merge with another and ultimately about unification with the divine.

Our greatest desire is to return to the source of all existence, with its unconditional love, bliss and peace. We seek out another being who brings these feelings of love, joy and contentment into our consciousness. When we find this special person, we want to hold on to them as we feel so much pleasure. Our belief is that the feelings we experience around this other being come from our beloved. Yet, we forget that our feelings are our own and that our beloved is merely the catalyst that helps us experience the love and joy contained within. When we look to quench our thirst from within, we uncover our fountain of self-love, joy and contentment. It becomes apparent that what we are seeking has been within us all along. Peace washes over us like a soft mist and our quest for external validation dissolves.

Our desires grow out of the stories we tell ourselves about what it will be like when we fulfill our aspirations. These stories are based on recurring thoughts we have of some future event. The future is always based on a fantasy and can

---

[57] Scientific American, How Important is Physical Contact with your Infant, Katherine Harmon, May 6, 2010 https://www.scientificamerican.com/article/infant-touch/

never be fulfilled because our future desires are always in the distance, like a carrot on a stick. Desire is always future focused. Happiness, joy and contentment can only be found in the present moment, not in the future and not in the past.

When fulfilling our desire leaves us wanting, it is the perfect moment to look at the underlying beliefs we have about our desires. Exploring our dissatisfaction allows us to turn toward that which will truly bring us greater happiness and peace. We begin to see how our desires, more often than not, lead us away from being content. Exploring our desires with conscious awareness as they arise allows us to clearly see what is truly important to us and what will bring us greater joy and peace.

There are times we both knowingly and unknowingly stoke the flames of our desire. We keep watering the seeds of desire, enabling them to grow deep roots and strengthen their hold over us. Our indulgence feeds their power and can create tangled vines of confusion that hide our core beliefs, preventing us from unravelling their grip on our consciousness. Sexual desire is one of these strongly held forces we typically keep hidden, not just from ourselves but from others as well. Undoubtedly, there are strong biological and hormonal factors that intensify this desire. Innate to each of us is the need to reproduce.

Beyond procreation, uncontrolled sexual desire can result in actions we would not normally take. Inappropriate comments, unwanted solicitation or comments towards another person, or risky sexual activity can be outcomes of indulged sexual desire. At the same time, suppressing our feelings only creates inner pressure and can lead to longer-term health issues. Being aware of which seeds of yearning we decide to nurture or not, determines the intensity of our desires. Whatever desire we water grows in our consciousness. Some desires we may want to nurture, such as love and compassion for all beings. Others we may want to weed out, such as the need for aggression, power and control. We can only see our ingrained desires when we willingly and consciously turn toward them. Otherwise, they run our lives unchecked and unchallenged. Awareness is the first step in recognizing that our desires may have greater control over us than perhaps we realized. Inner peace and ultimate happiness can only surface when we are willing to look into our desires and selectively water the seeds of contentment.

Turning toward our desire and diving into our thoughts and feelings with conscious awareness reveals deep-rooted beliefs that prevent us from experiencing inner peace. Exploring our desires creates the opportunity to remove the barriers that prevent us from experiencing contentment and joy. When our desires surface, our focus often becomes about satisfying our longing. It is as if there is an itch we simply must scratch.

Alternatively, we need to be aware of and notice our desires. It is often helpful to name them. For example, "This is my desire for material things" or "I am noticing my longing for companionship" or "My sexual desire is dominating my thoughts right now." Once named, our practice becomes about letting go of our need to satisfy the itch. At the root of these and all our desires is a deep-seated belief that we need this thing or person in order to be happy. Being present with and willing to look at these hidden perspectives allows us to begin to see the ways in which we use external gratification to try and satisfy our internal desire.

We cannot fill an inner void through external acquisitions. It is our beliefs that must be challenged as they are the illusions that have us believe we are lacking in some way. The belief we need something or someone to make us happy is erroneous. Happiness comes from within. There is no relationship, job, material possession or wealth that can provide ongoing happiness and contentment. Just like in meditation, we return again and again to look at our unconscious desires so we can release ourselves from the bondage of their shackles and awaken to the inner peace and joy that is ever present in the moment. The dance of dynamic peace is forever undulating between the pull of desire and bliss of inner peace.

Undoubtedly, some of our desires are intense and well-anchored in our being. It can be challenging to face them and to let them go. Yet, just like in meditation, we repeatedly return to wash away our limiting perspective. When we catch ourselves indulging our desires, we must not be judgemental or critical toward ourselves. We can simply notice, name it and let go in whatever way we can, slowly chipping away at our limiting viewpoint. In the process, we begin to more frequently experience moments of inner peace and tranquility. Our view of the world changes as we change. We become more loving and compassionate toward ourselves with each new surrender, and in turn have greater capacity to be loving, kind and compassionate toward all beings.

Practical application

To apply what you have learned in this section, try one or two of the suggestions below. Take a step, test the water or jump in with both feet. The choice is yours.

Take a step:

- What is a desire you have fulfilled in the past? How satisfied were you when you achieved/attained it?

- Notice when your desires take you into a future fantasy and out of the present moment.

Test the water:

- What are your desires and what is the perceived void you are trying to fulfill? Listen to the storyline running in your head. Challenge yourself to let go of the story.

- What are areas of dissatisfaction in your life? Look into your expectations and beliefs about how things should be. Identify and name your desire. Let go of the judgement or criticism.

Jump in with both feet:

- What are your secret desires? How much do they influence how you think and act? Identify the actions you are taking as a result of your desires. Decide whether to continue these actions or let some or all of them go. What changes as a result?

- What desires do you keep fanning the flames of? How is this contributing to your suffering? Let go of something that stokes the flames of desire.

Passion

> *The desire for true happiness is nothing to feel ashamed about.*
> ~ Thanissaro Bhikkhu

Knowing ourselves also includes knowing and resolutely following our passions in life. Passion is any compelling emotion or feeling, such as love. Desire is to wish or long for, to crave or want.[58] Passions are the passageways to living a fulfilling and joyous life. They are the call of our soul and the footpaths to the top of the mountain. We may have many passions, or a few specific ones we are drawn towards. Some passions are easier to identify, such as connection with family or being in the outdoors. Other passions, we may discover, are only hints to a bigger calling. In some cases, we follow our passions only to find we have made a wrong turn that leaves us feeling unsatisfied and unfulfilled. Knowing ourselves means also looking beneath our passions to see what is driving us. In so doing, we uncover our true passions and begin to live a life that is filled with greater joy, happiness and contentment.

We are constantly learning about ourselves through the people, activities and things that bring us joy. From an early age, we carry with us unique aptitudes and abilities that are inherent to our passions. There are many examples of people who are born with natural gifts in music, sports, philosophy and art, but each of us brings distinct abilities into the world that make us who we are. The passions we have point us in a direction we follow keenly. While some

---

[58] Dictionary.com

follow one path in life, others may take many roads in the pursuit of their passion. Each pathway leads to greater self-discovery and insight.

We leverage our passion in finding and creating careers for ourselves, hoping to spend years doing what we love, but passions may also change as we learn and grow. We may be a world-renowned musician who finds teaching to be our true passion. One pathway leads to another as our passions are not static but rather dynamic. My teacher, Master Charles Cannon, often said, "Follow your bliss." When we trust in and fervently follow our passions, we experience inner contentment and joy. Our lives become richer and we feel a sense of fulfilment.

Some passions are apparent and easy to recognize while others are only glimpses into greater callings. Our likes and dislikes are some of the initial indicators for us of those pathways that lead to greater happiness. For some, their preferences are quite apparent and they easily walk down a path with enthusiasm. For example, some feel passionately called to be a doctor, dancer, teacher or entertainer. Others feel less passionate about any one direction, leaving them unsure of what route to take in their life. They can become frozen in doubt or fear and unwilling to choose a direction. Additionally, there may be times when our beliefs can get in the way of our passions, causing us to veer away from those things that excite us. When we have conflicting ideas about our passions and our ability to sustain the lifestyle of our dreams, we may choose a direction that provides safety and security over taking a leap of faith. This was the case for me.

From a very young age, I wanted to be a professional dancer. I studied ballet from the age of four under the guidance of my local dance teacher. I had great opportunities at the National Ballet School of Canada and with the founders of the Royal Winnipeg Ballet at their new school in the interior of British Columbia. However, I carried a belief that it would not be a financially sustainable lifestyle despite my natural abilities. As a result, I gave up on my passion in my early teenage years. Maybe your passion is be to professional tennis player, but you believe your chances of success are limited. Our fear or hesitation dampens our enthusiasm and we feel doubtful of our success. Yet, choosing a path out of fear and trepidations may lead to a life of limited fulfilment and joy.

There may be times when we follow our dreams but are swayed to take a different path because of a perceived benefit or reward. You love your job but want to have more income, so you take on a new role, luring you away from the very thing that brings you the most joy and happiness. Similarly, we may believe we are following our bliss only to realize down the road that we have taken the wrong path. If we follow our passions with faith and courage, we will ultimately find greater fulfillment and joy in our lives. Our commitment to following our passion is one of the most supportive things we can do to continually experience inner peace.

It is equally important to look underneath our passions to discover what is driving us to act. Is it out of a need to be of service? Are we looking for recognition or acknowledgement? What level of satisfaction will you have if you fulfill your passion? Our passions always take us towards something. Learning what motivates us helps us peel back the obscure layers of our consciousness to find our true self. Often what we find when we look deep into ourselves is a need to feel joy, happiness and self-love. We all want to return to our true nature: a state of peace, love and compassion. Our passions are the roadways that lead us home. Like a magnet, we are drawn toward our essence, and ultimately we are unable to escape its pull.

Consider the greatest passions in your life. Close your eyes and take three slow deep breaths. Then turn your awareness toward your passions and look behind them to see what thoughts and feelings are hidden there. Notice the joy and happiness they bring to your life. Feel the warmth and contentment they provide you. Observe the sense of inner peace and bliss that resides in this place. Following your bliss leads you home to yourself and you soon realize that "what you were looking for is what is looking."[59]

We must all find a way to bring our passions to life. Follow the roads that spark your curiosity and inspire you to leap instead of walk. Be still enough to notice the twists and turns in the road and to know which roads have signs showing you the way home. There may be times when we feel doubt and hesitation. In these moments, we need to stay committed to our path and always remain the watchful observer, just like a captain steering his ship towards the shore. Listen to the calm inner voice that speaks to you and question those that say it should be other than it is. A quote by Martin Luther King Jr. speaks to these moments of uncertainty: "Take the first step in faith. You don't have

---

[59] MonkeySocietyBlog, What you are looking for is what is looking, attributed to St. Francis of Assisi, October 26, 2012 http://monkeysocietyblog.blogspot.com/2012/10/what-you-are-looking-for-is-what-is.html

to see the whole staircase, just take the first step."[60] When we follow our passion, we may not know where the path is taking us. All we have to do is take the next step and allow the pathway to reveal itself.

Practical application

To apply what you have learned in this section, try one or two of the suggestions below. Take a step, test the water or jump in with both feet. The choice is yours.

Take a step:

- List your unique aptitudes and abilities. Others may have similar ones but no one can deliver them like you. Which ones have you followed and which ones call to you still?

- What has your inner voice been saying that calls to you to make a change in your life? How can you embrace this voice and take action?

Test the water:

- What is the current path you are on and is it fulfilling, joyous and rewarding? If not, what change/action do you need to take to move you in this direction?

---

[60] Good Reads, Martin Luther King Jr./Quotes/Quotable Quotes https://www.goodreads.com/quotes/199214-take-the-first-step-in-faith-you-don-t-have-to

Choose one thing you can do now to move toward greater joy and peace.

- Have you been swayed away from your passion(s)? If so, what has caused you to divert from your passion? Is this new direction bringing you happiness and fulfilment? Decide to make one change in your life that will move you in the direction or your passion.

Jump in with both feet:

- What passion are you afraid to follow and why? What is the belief or perspective that is holding you back? Commit to not letting your fear hold you back and decide to trust in your inner calling. Take one step toward your passion.

- If you could take a leap of faith to greater joy and inner peace, what would it be? Take one action that moves you closer to fulfilling your passion. What if you were just to leap? What story do you make up about how things would be? Commit to taking action now.

The mirror

It is because it is empty that the mirror reflects an image.
~ Wang Tong

How we see the world is based on the lens through which we view it. If we change our lens, our view of the world shifts. Consider how different the view of the earth is from a plane flying at 20,000 feet versus from the space station. In a similar way, our perception of ourselves and the world creates our reality.

Albert Einstein said, "Reality is merely an illusion, albeit a very persistent one." Most of us view the world from a dualistic perspective. We see ourselves as unique and separate from all other manifested phenomenon. Yet, mystics and spiritual teachers view the world differently, from a perspective of nondualism where there is no separation between self and other. Everything is the expression of one energy, one source. The world we experience reflects our thoughts, feelings and beliefs. In this way, the outer world is a mirror of what is going on inside of us. Seeing our reflection constantly being reflected back to us can be uplifting and can also be challenging to face. When we see love and compassion in our world, we are seeing our own love and compassion reflected back to us. When we see anger and suffering in our world, we see our own inner anger and suffering. Being willing to truthfully look at and contemplate on our reflections with conscious awareness takes courage. Only when we are willing to own and be accountable for our reality can we experience peace and happiness in our lives.

The world we experience on a day-to-day basis is founded on our perception of reality. The thoughts, feelings and beliefs we hold are the filters through which we see the world. If we believe the world is nurturing and loving, our perception of the world will reflect back to us this point of view. Perhaps you have a friend who always sees the positive in every situation, regardless of the circumstances. The lens through which they see the world is polarized with a positive perspective. Similarly, during challenging times, we believe the world should be different than how it is unfolding in the moment. Maybe you have lost your job and feel devastated. Yet, you later realize it was a blessing as it freed you up to find a more rewarding job that better aligned with your values and skillset.

Our minds love to categorize and organize the world in order to maintain a degree of control. We often seek out similar viewpoints in the world that validate our beliefs and, ironically, our perception has been fine tuned to find them. When we encounter something or someone that provides an alternate perspective to ours, we become confused or discount it as not being true. Realizing our view of things is just one perspective among many divergent viewpoints enables us to be open and receptive to new possibilities. Perhaps you believe people are innately kind and caring toward others. Yet, you feel bewildered and outraged by the inhumane treatment inflicted by humans on each other around the world. We cannot see the intense, internal suffering of others that results in their cruel actions. Only through seeking to understanding someone's anguish can we hope to understand their motives.

Recognizing that our perspective is just one way of looking at things enables us to consider that the world is perhaps different than we believe it to be. When we seek to understand, we open ourselves up to greater peace and contentment. Continually looking to see the world as it is and not as we perceive it through our distorted lens, provides true insight and understanding.

Most people view the world from a dualistic perspective. We see ourselves as autonomous from all manifested phenomenon. We hold the belief that there is a subject (ourselves) and an object (everything outside of ourselves). As such, we build up a belief system that supports our separateness and which is reinforced through our interactions in the world. We look at a tree and see it as a solid structure with a trunk, branches and leaves. It is separate from us and not part of our physical make up. Thus, we see it as something outside of ourselves that we observe despite the fact that our perspective is based on our limited vision in terms of the range of colour, light, magnification and ultraviolet spectrum. Everything and everyone is viewed in the same way, from a perspective that only sees distinctiveness. It is as if we are a drop of ocean water that maintains its uniqueness from the rest of the ocean. As such, we are an individual within the human race. We may see ourselves as part of a collective race, ethnic group, nation and/or gender but we still consider ourselves to be solitary. From this dualistic perspective we maintain an isolationist viewpoint. We can never merge or be with another because we are always distinct.

Duality implies we are always alone in the world, yet we long to merge with another. For so many, our spousal relationships are our most direct attempt to unite with our world. Two people come together united in working and acting as one. Our physical intimacy is the closest we ever come to actually merging. Yet, even the act of sexual intercourse is not everlasting and can often be performed from a perspective of individual gratification. There can be no lasting peace and tranquility found in a dualistic perspective of the world. Only by seeing the world as a reflection of our thoughts, feelings and beliefs can true reality unfold around us and within us simultaneously and inter-dependently.

A non-dualistic perspective of reality means we see the world and everything in it as interconnected and interdependent. Ancient teachers and mystics throughout the ages have always known and taught about the interdependence of all manifested and unmanifested phenomenon. Using the analogy of a tree again, from a non-dualistic perspective, it has a trunk, branches and leaves, but it also is dynamic energy made up of atoms, neutrons, protons and electrons dancing together in the form of a tree. These elements are in the air, the water and in us moving and interacting in and amongst all life. We are not separate from a tree but a part of it at levels that we simply cannot see with our eyes.

In his book *Ageless Body Timeless Mind* Deepak Chopra writes about viewing one's hand under a powerful microscope, revealing deeper and deeper layers of matter until eventually what is left is the space between matter. Hence, we are not as dense as we believe ourselves to be. Rather we are dancing molecules, similar to the tree, interacting with all life visible and invisible to the naked eye.

When viewed from the perspective of non-dualism, the external world reflects our internal world and vice versa. The suffering of another being reflects our own suffering. The love we feel for another is the love that is found within us. We are all reflections of each other. As a result, our reflections also show us what is going on inside ourselves when we pause to look within. When someone is angry, it can bring up our own anger. When I began to view all interactions with the world as a reflection of what was going on inside of me, I realized that each moment, each person was a learning opportunity into myself. The dance of dynamic peace was revealing itself to me, and I could use the insights gained to create greater peace in my life. Looking within gives us the opportunity to discover and explore our own issues.

The perspective that we hold about ourselves and the world shifts when we view the world from a more truthful non-dualistic viewpoint. Rather than isolation, we see interconnectedness. We may be a drop in the ocean of consciousness but we are also a part of the ocean. The love and compassion we show towards others reflect the love and compassion we have within ourselves. By creating greater inner peace and serenity within our being, we are also creating greater peace and tranquility throughout the world.

From a non-dualistic perspective, we must be willing to look at our reflection in the mirror to see ourselves more truthfully. When we see something or someone we do not like, we need to explore what it is within ourselves that we are not accepting. Perhaps you do not like the way a work colleague socializes with the leaders in your organization. Do you hold the belief that they should not mingle with leaders? Are you judging yourself for not being willing to get to know the organization's leaders? Maybe you believe your colleague is socializing with the leaders to get a promotion and you disagree with their methods. In a similar way, we may agree with the views held by a friend or family member despite the fact their perspective may not be liked by everyone. What is it that you believe others may not agree with? Is your point of view right and theirs is wrong? Exploring our own thoughts, feelings and beliefs about situations that create a reaction in us allows us to understand our own limiting perspectives. It takes great courage and personal self-awareness to be willing to look at our underlying beliefs rather than simply being reactive.

The world is truly our mirror constantly reflecting back to us the perspectives that we hold. If we do not like our reflections, we need to explore what is going on internally with us so we can let go of our limiting viewpoints. As such, we must also hold ourselves accountable for the impact we have on the world. If our impact is not what we intended it to be, then we need to look at our underlying beliefs, expectations or agendas. Non-dualism requires a conscious awareness of events and situations moment to moment. We must understand that the dance of dynamic peace is our own dance with consciousness. We need to own whatever is happening in our lives from the perspective that we are creating it. As the creator, we can change our world simply by changing our point of view. Peace and joy are found as we peel away the unending layers of our unconsciousness. Meditation, self-study and ongoing reflection are the tools we use to help us let go of our dualistic perspective, so we can live in a state of inner peace.

Practical application

To apply what you have learned in this section, try one or two of the suggestions below. Take a step, test the water or jump in with both feet. The choice is yours.

Take a step:

- Sit quietly and try to step back to observe your behaviours and actions. Write out what your belief(s) are by which you view the world (e.g., what's right, wrong, good, bad about the world). Is there anything that surprises you?

- Consider the possibility that all life is interconnected. All living things are dependent on everything else. How does your view of the world change/shift?

Test the water:

- Consider those things/events that you consider challenging in the world. What is your perspective of the world that keeps it challenging? What's an alternative perspective to consider? Push yourself to do something you find challenging.

- Do you view the world from a dualistic or non-dualistic perspective? What situations do you view from a dualistic perspective? For those things or people that you view from a dualistic perspective, look for at least one thing that points to our interconnectedness.

Jump in with both feet:

- At times when you feel isolated from the world or people, notice your degree of suffering. What's the view of the world that you hold and what needs to change? Challenge your limiting viewpoint and take action to make positive changes in your life.

- When do you feel the most connected with life? What is your level of inner peace and joy? Do one thing daily that keeps you connected to life.

Kindness

> *Kindness in words creates confidence.*
> *Kindness in thinking creates profoundness.*
> *Kindness in giving creates love.*
> *~Tao Te Ching*

Our inner peace and happiness are expressed by the kindness we have toward ourselves and all beings. Kindness is the water that nourishes understanding, compassion and love. It is expressed in our thoughts, words and actions. When we perform acts of kindness, our spirit soars and we experience bliss. We feel more connected to our true selves when we are kind-hearted and considerate. Acts of kindness have the power to alleviate suffering. There is so much unhappiness and anguish in the world today that could be lessened by simply being kinder to one another. Unconditional kindness elevates our consciousness and the spirit of humanity. Contentment and joy fill our being and we are miraculously enriched through the experience of being kind.

Kindness flows out of our ability to be consciously aware of the need for empathy in the present moment. We could not be kind toward ourselves or other beings if we were not able to see beyond our egocentric self. Kindness requires that we rise above our self-focus and indulgences to see beyond our singular viewpoint. We must be present, in the here and now, in order to experience kind-heartedness. In moments of kindness, our humanity fills us and we feel a greater connection to all life. Being kind opens the doorway to understanding and compassion. We become more willing to let go of our conditional thinking to express our empathy.

Perhaps you feel compelled to help a friend in need. Maybe you donate to a global children's charity to alleviate suffering around the world. Possibly you give your time to saving our global forests. Acts of kindness do not have to be grand or touch millions of lives. We could easily be more kind toward ourselves, resulting in greater self-love. We may take in a stray animal to give it a good home. We may smile at a stranger as we pass them on the street. Unreserved acts of kindness fill our being with peace and happiness. Research suggests that "one good deed would make you happier, and the happier you feel, the more likely you are to do another kind act."[61] We are more peaceful and compassionate when we act with kindness. Our lives are enriched and we experience a sense of peace and joy within our being.

Kindness first gains expression in the thoughts we have about ourselves and other beings. The reality we hold about ourselves and the world is based on our perspective. Change our perception and we change the world. When we think kindly of ourselves and other people, we feel greater harmony and contentment. If we harbour unkind thoughts, our world is filled with negativity and bitterness. We feel less joy and peace. When we cultivate kind thoughts, we soften our perspective and see the good all around us. Our hearts open toward ourselves and to other people. The artificial barriers we put up and spend so much time maintaining begin to dissolve, leaving room for kindness to unfold. When we nurture kind thoughts they grow in strength and breadth.

---

[61] Greater Good Magazine, Science Based Insights for a Meaningful Life, Kindness Makes you Happy and Happiness Makes you Kind, Alex Dixon, September 6, 2011 https://greatergood.berkeley.edu/article/item/kindness_makes_you_happy_and_happiness_makes_you_kind/

What we put out into our world is reflected back to us in equal or amplified measure. Being centered in kindness, we energetically emit kindness to all beings. Kindness, in its purest form, is given unconditionally without need for anything or benefit in return. It pours out of our love for self and others. Harbouring kind thoughts, we experience greater self-love, compassion and ultimately inner peace.

Consciously choosing to use words that express kindness grounds our kind-heartedness, while simultaneously promoting receptivity and openness in others. When we speak with anger, aggression or vengefulness we may provoke a fight or flight response in others. Our negativity is reciprocated back to us through the response of others. Electing to use words that demonstrate kindness allows others to be less reactive and more receptive to what is being said. At the core of being kind is the fundamental perspective of acceptance and non-judgement. Perhaps you want to vent your frustration toward a work colleague for their perceived incompetence, but instead you use words to seek understanding and insight. Maybe you feel angry waiting in line at the store but decide to speak kindly with the teller who is struggling to serve customers as fast as possible. Our words have the ability to strike blows or to melt away barriers.

Our close and intimate relationships, with a spouse, parents or children, are some of the most challenging situations to always approach from a place of kindness. We feel we can let our guard down and speak freely to those closest to us. Yet, the words we choose to express ourselves can deepen or destroy relationships. These relationships contain a history that can unduly influence our ability to be kind. Yet, it is these close relationships where kindness is frequently most needed. Likewise, in the workplace, leaders or colleagues fail to speak kindly, creating toxic environments. We believe it is important to give feedback to others and yet seldom do we consider doing so with kindness.

Some of the most challenging times to be kind are in moments of anger. Typically anger arises out of a belief that we have been wronged, threatened or hurt in some way. It can be challenging to pause and reflect on the roots of our anger before we respond. Still, acts of kindness when we are angry can have far greater impact than reacting out of our anger. When we take the time to be present and look underneath our anger, we see someone who is hurting. Expressing our true feelings with vulnerability opens doors versus slamming them shut. Our inner peace and serenity are impacted positively or negatively through the words we use and the kind-hearted intention behind them. When we speak with kindness, our world becomes more harmonious and tranquil.

Acting with kindness toward ourselves and other beings creates a world based on kind-heartedness and compassion. John Pym, an English parliamentarian from the sixteenth century said, "Actions are more precious than words." Today we use the common colloquialism "actions speak louder than words." Experience has taught us that people's words can sometimes be empty, so we look to their demonstrated action to really know what they believe and stand for. Acts of kindness carry weight and can influence others to act.

In 1995, the Random Acts of Kindness Foundation was founded in California. It is dedicated to conducting quiet **acts** of **kindness** and generosity in our communities. Similarly,

World Kindness Day is celebrated annually on November thirteenth around the globe. There is a growing movement to perform random acts of kindness raising all of humanity. Everything we do has an impact on those around us, in our communities and globally. When we act with kindness, there is ripple effect that permeates outward.

There are unlimited acts of kindness we can perform. In the workplace, maybe you bring someone a cup of coffee. You surprise your spouse with flowers or a day at the spa. Maybe you buy a lunch for a random street person. Walking by a homeless person covered and laying on the street with a sign asking for food compelled me to buy him a meal. The joy in his face filled my being with a sense of kind-hearted peace. Kind acts are not just an idea or words, but rather a beacon that has the ability to lift our spirits and reconnect us with our humanity. When we act with unconditional kindness, we experience a sense of contentment and joy. Our actions show compassion and love for another being and we in turn feel the warm glow of our kind-heartedness.

When kindness fills our thoughts, words and actions there is a benevolent quality to our being. How we see the world and how the world views us is with compassion and love. Inwardly, we feel greater peace and tranquility. There is less struggle to achieve or obtain and more focus on being and giving. Being kind enables us to awaken to our true nature: one of gentleness, empathy and profound love for ourselves and all beings. As the ebb and flow of dynamic peace unfolds, kindness anchors us in inner peace. So much more is possible when we approach life and all beings with kindness. Our inner peace and contentment are revealed through the kindness we express, and we are enriched exponentially as a result of our kindness.

Practical application

To apply what you have learned in this section, try one or two of the suggestions below. Take a step, test the water or jump in with both feet. The choice is yours.

Take a step:

- Notice if your actions arise out of kindness and openness, or if they originate in anger and contraction.
- Perform a random act of kindness and notice your impact. What is the impact on others? What is the impact on you?

Test the water:

- What is one way you could be more kind to yourself? Use kinder thoughts and words when talking to yourself.
- In moments of anger, pause and decide to speak truthfully but with kindness in your heart. What is your impact?

Jump in with both feet:

- Perform one random act of kindness each day for a week. Notice how you feel and what your impact is.
- Become a champion for kindness in the world. Promote World Kindness Day. Sponsor a random act of kindness day at work or in your community.

Compassion

> *When you have learned compassion for yourself,*
> *compassion for others is automatic.*
> *~ Henepola Gunaratana*

Developing and displaying compassion for ourselves and all beings nurtures our inner peace. Most of us innately feel compassion for others when we see the suffering caused by natural disasters and tragedies. Yet, true compassion begins first and foremost when we learn to be compassionate toward ourselves.

We learn to be compassionate when we treat ourselves with kindness despite our self-judgements or when we fail or regret our actions. As we become more compassionate with ourselves, we have greater capacity to be compassionate toward other beings. We can understand and empathize with others who have struggled just as we have. We want to lift their suffering.

When we learn to be more compassionate, we care more for the rights of all beings, including animals, plants and the earth. There is an honouring of the divine nature within us and all life. Being compassionate softens our hearts, and we become open to that which is present in the moment. When we are compassionate, calm and serenity wash over our being and we feel greater inner contentment. Compassion allows us to be less judgemental and critical of ourselves as we move through the ongoing dance of dynamic peace.

Our ability to be compassionate grows as we develop our capacity to be compassionate toward ourselves. During times of struggle and challenge, being able to look at ourselves with tenderness and acceptance fosters self-compassion. We are more caring for ourselves when we are sick and healing. Our ability to be patient and gentle with ourselves grows. There is a sense of acceptance of whatever is happening in each moment. When we have compassion for ourselves, we are more willing to look at the judgemental thoughts of ourselves that we harbour. Thoughts that we are not smart enough, quick enough or good enough surface for everyone. Yet, these thoughts hold less weight and have less of an impact on us when we have developed the ability to be compassionate. In recognizing our judgemental thoughts, we see how harsh and critical our thoughts can be and we begin to question their validity. We can be so disapproving of ourselves taking away our joy and peace. Compassion means we are accepting of our humanness and perceived imperfections.

Compassion leads to wisdom and greater wisdom leads to greater compassion. Each of the qualities of wisdom and compassion nurture and expand on each other. We can rest in the knowing that we love ourselves just as we are. At times when we are feeling vulnerable and scared, compassion softens our fears and we are able to accept our vulnerability with openness and gentleness. Having compassion for ourselves means we see all of our flaws and we still love and accept ourselves. As we are less at odds within ourselves, we are able to experience more profound inner peace and tranquility.

Our capacity to be compassionate toward others increases the more we are compassionate with ourselves. It is difficult to give what we do not have. Trying to be compassionate toward another being is challenging when we are unable to be compassionate toward ourselves. It is like trying to get water out of an empty well. If we can fill our inner well with compassion, we are better able to be compassionate toward all beings. We see our own imperfections in others and we experience empathy and sympathy for them. We make fewer assumptions and judgements of other people. Just as we care about ourselves, we also care for the wellbeing of all life. As our wisdom and compassion grows, we begin to include all human and non-human beings in the embrace of our compassion. Our capacity to care for the animals, plants and Mother Earth increases as we feel a connection with all beings. There is a reverence for all life that unfolds within us as we expand our awareness and ability to be compassionate. We begin to see the divine in everything and everyone.

Compassion opens our heart to life. We experience joy and peace in our being when we are compassionate. Something magical occurs when we stop being self-absorbed and feel compassion for others. Somehow our own ability to be kind-hearted grows. Our well of compassion increases and we are enriched in the process. Being compassionate brings us into the present moment. Our thoughts shift from the past or the future to the here and now. We awaken to the bliss of the moment and feel peace and tranquility fill our being. The Buddha taught over 2,500 years ago that to reach a state of enlightenment (a grand word that means fundamental happiness[62]) we must develop compassion and wisdom. Compassion and wisdom are often referred to as two wings working together, enabling us to fly.[63] Wisdom that sees truthfully combined with compassion that sees

---

[62] True Happiness, Pema Chodron, Sounds True 2006
[63] ThoughtCo, Buddhism and Compassion, Barbara O'Brien, July 9, 2018
https://www.thoughtco.com/buddhism-and-compassion-449719

our oneness enables us to be in a state of inner peace. The ebb and flow of wisdom and compassion enables us to be more present in the dance of dynamic peace.

Compassion dissolves the illusory walls we have built up around our hearts. There is far too little compassion in today's corporate, materialistic and capitalistic world. We have lost the sense of a shared community and interdependence necessary for the survival of all beings. The following parable illustrates our need to be caring and compassionate toward one another: [64]

> One day a man said to God, "God, I would like to know what Heaven and Hell are like."
>
> God showed the man two doors. Behind the first one was a room. In the middle of the room was a large round table with a large pot of stew. It smelled delicious and made the man's mouth water, but the people sitting around the table holding spoons were thin and sickly. They appeared to be famished. None of them could reach into the pot of stew and take a spoonful because the handles on their spoons were longer than their arms. They could not get the spoons back into their mouths.

---

[64] Meant To Be Happy, Character & Values, Allegory of The Long Spoons http://meanttobehappy.com/allegory-of-the-long-spoons-how-to-make-heaven-on-earth

The man shuddered at the sight of their misery and suffering. God said, "You have seen Hell."

Behind the second door was a room that appeared exactly the same as the first one. There was the large round table with the large pot of wonderful stew that made the man's mouth water. The people had the same long-handled spoons, but they were well nourished and plump, laughing and talking.

The man said, "I don't understand."

God smiled. "It is simple," he said. "Love only requires one skill. These people learned early on to share and feed one another. The greedy only think of themselves."

Compassion is about caring and nurturing one another. It is about seeing the suffering of another being (human, animal or our planet) and acting in a way to alleviate their suffering, such as through a kind word, the sharing of a meal, or donating time or money. We must learn to feed one another, to comfort one another in times of sorrow, and to seek to understand rather than building walls, starting wars or committing genocide. Even holding compassionate thoughts alters everything because our ability to create change begins with our thinking. Through our compassion toward ourselves and others, we can experience greater inner peace and happiness, not just for ourselves but for all beings.

Practical application

To apply what you have learned in this section, try one or two of the suggestions below. Take a step, test the water or jump in with both feet. The choice is yours.

Take a step:

- Observe times when you feel compassion for another being and when you don't. What insight do you gain about yourself?

- When is it difficult for you to be compassionate and what belief or perspective do you hold to be true?

Test the water:

- In what areas of your life do you need to be more compassionate towards yourself? Do one thing to be more self-compassionate right now?

- Notice times when you are critical or judgemental of others. What would a more compassionate perspective look like? Let go of your judgement and focus upon loving yourself.

Jump in with both feet:

- Recognize your self-critical flaws and/or imperfections. Write them out and then try to re-write them in a more loving and compassionate way.

- Think of at least two ways you could be more compassionate in the workplace. Commit to one or more and take action. What is your impact?

Gratitude

Let us look at a humble virtue, that of gratitude.
With this virtue alone, the world could be at peace.
~ Buddhadasa Bhikkhu

When we fill our life with gratitude, we experience inner contentment and peace. Our life becomes joyous and celebratory. Gratitude shifts our focus from a perspective of scarcity to one of abundance. We see the richness of life and feel grateful for the abundance that life offers. During challenging or difficult times, being grateful for the fundamentals of life reminds us what is truly important, such as the air we breathe, the water we drink and the love of those close to us.

When we feel disappointment or frustration over the things that we do not have, it is helpful to remind ourselves of the precious things that fill our lives. Gratitude always lifts our spirit and softens our inner struggles. There is always something that we can be grateful for regardless of the circumstances. A perspective of gratitude acts like a magnet drawing greater abundance towards us. Living in a more consistent state of gratitude allows us to experience peace and joy in every moment.

There are times in our lives when we feel unhappy, as if life is in some way not providing us with the joy and pleasure we expect. Our focus is on what we do not have, while we give little attention to the good in our lives. For instance, we may not have enough money and feel we are always struggling. The high demands of our job does not allow enough time for family and friends. We want greater intimacy and connection with our spouse. In these moments, when we shift our focus towards gratitude, our perspective changes, and we begin to see abundance where there was scarcity. We become grateful for the money that we have in our lives. There is recognition that money does not buy happiness, and we begin to notice those things that are truly creating joy in our life. We are thankful we have a job which sustains us. We acknowledge that not everyone has a job, and we are fortunate to be working. We feel thankful we have a committed relationship in our lives. As a result, we begin to express more love and appreciation for our loved one, which begins to be reciprocated by our spouse. When we change our viewpoint to one of gratitude, our world correspondingly changes. Whatever we focus on in our lives grows. When we focus on scarcity, scarcity grows. When we focus on gratitude, our lives become more abundant. Reflecting daily on all that we have to be grateful for brings greater peace and joy, while simultaneously enriching our life with greater abundance.

We are often confused about the things we need versus the things that we want. Typically, our wants exceed our needs and we focus on what is lacking. A want, in and of itself, points to a deficit between how we see ourselves and what we aspire to be. When we focus on what we want, we are always future focused and never in the present moment. Our wants can only be fulfilled at some future point because they are never found in the here and now. A want is a longing, a desire for things to be other than how we find them. Perhaps you want new furniture, or a new car or career. In some way, we have entwined our happiness with the fulfillment of our want. We can challenge ourselves to look at our wants with conscious awareness and ask how the achievement of our desire will bring us greater happiness and peace. When we buy that new furniture, how will it increase our joy in life?

At the core of our wants is a belief that the attainment of our desire will bring us contentment. Yet, where does contentment and happiness come from? True happiness comes from within. It can not be bought, acquired, purchased or bartered for. When we seek external gratification to be happy, we will undoubtedly find ourselves feeling dissatisfied and disappointed. Rather, when we focus on what we have and feel gratitude for it, our lives are so much more enriched. At a fundamental level, without air to breathe nothing else matters. Without water to drink and food to eat, we could not survive. If we did not have shelter from the elements we could perish. Deprived of human contact, we may experience depression and lose touch with reality. Gratitude for the basics of life remind us that so much of what we need is provided. The air we breathe, the water we drink, the food we eat and the companionship of others are found within our surroundings. When our wants seem to consume our consciousness, reminding ourselves of the basic needs of life and how they are abundantly provided helps us to reaffirm what is truly important in our lives. Gratitude alleviates the hold that our wants have on us and enables us to experience moments of peace and tranquility. We begin to see abundance where there was deficiency.

We always have something we can be grateful for in our lives: the smile of a dear friend; the warmth of the sun, and the glory of a clear blue sky; the embrace of a loved one; a refreshing drink of cool water or the delicious taste of a fresh strawberry. Throughout our day, there are numerous things we can be grateful for at home, work or play. To experience gratitude, we only need to turn our attention towards those things and people in our lives that we feel appreciation for.

The need for gratitude is not a new phenomenon. The Buddha spoke of being thankful over two-and-a-half-millennia ago.

> *Let us rise up and be thankful,*
> *for if we didn't learn a lot today, at least we learned a little,*
> *and if we didn't learn a little, at least we didn't get sick,*
> *and if we got sick, at least we didn't die;*
> *so, let us all be thankful.*
> ~ Buddha

Gratitude draws us to the present moment where peace and contentment fill our being. The experience of truly living can only be found in the present moment. The past is gone and the future is always some illusory fantasy. Only in this very moment can we say that we are alive. Gratitude is about what we are experiencing here and now. It is the same place where happiness, joy and peace reside. Whenever I am struggling or feeling down, I look to what I am grateful for in this moment. Before falling asleep at night, I often remind myself of what I am grateful for today. I feel grateful for my good health, my family, my home, my friends, and the bounty provided me by Mother Nature. Joy and happiness always accompany my expressions of gratitude. When we are grateful for this moment and all the subsequent moments that follow, we have all that we need. We are at peace because there is no wanting. We have all we need, and it is enough.

Practical application

To apply what you have learned in this section, try one or two of the suggestions below. Take a step, test the water or jump in with both feet. The choice is yours.

Take a step:

- Notice if your focus is on what you think is lacking in your life or on what you are grateful for. Observe how your happiness grows when you feel gratitude.

- Notice how needs and wants are always future focused. Reflect on moments of gratitude and how they are always in the present moment.

Test the water:

- Make a list of all the things you are grateful for in your life.

- At times when you feel dissatisfied with life, make a list of everything you are grateful for.

Jump in with both feet:

- Before retiring for the night, think about or journal all the things you are grateful for today.

- When you acquire or achieve a need/want, notice how long you feel satisfied. Now make a list of all the people and things that bring you joy. Did your need/want make the list?

Unconditional love

> *Being deeply loved by someone gives you strength;*
> *loving someone deeply gives you courage.*
> *~ Lao-Tzu*

Unconditional love is the expression of our true nature. It arises out of our willingness to work through our judgements and desire, finding empathy through self-kindness and compassion. Our sense of gratitude fills our being, giving rise to unconditional love of self and others. Love touches us all deeply and reconnects us with the source of life.

Unconditional love has the ability to tear down barriers and mend fences. It can warm cold hearts and remove obstacles in our consciousness. Love can also be blind and can ignite incredible rage. Yet, we are all looking to be loved and to experience love, as if yearning to return home from a long journey. At the core of our being, we long to be accepted and loved by others but equally by ourselves. When we experience love, we want to hold on to it. Our belief is that love comes from an external source, our beloved, and we do not recognize that they are simply the mirror through which our own love is reflected back to us. Love is our natural expression when we are at peace within ourselves. Our cup overflows with radiant bliss and tranquility when we reside in love. Love transcends understanding as it is the true expression of our divine nature.

We are all looking to find unconditional love in one form or another throughout our lives. From the moment of birth, we need love in order to grow and mature. Throughout our life, we seek out a partner to love and who loves us back.

Even in old age, we need the love of our family and friends to feel joy and contentment. We write, sing, dialogue and create legends about love's triumphs and loves lost.

Our desire for love is based on our fundamental need to experience inner bliss and contentment. We are drawn towards love like the gravitational force of the planets. The pull is a force beyond our control and continues for eternity. True love is not about possession, lust or control. Rather it is the experience of tenderness, warmth and the enlivening of spirit within us. Most of us probably remember the excitement and anguish of our first love. We did not know we could be so captivated and awestruck at the same time. Love has no boundaries or barriers. It crosses all religious, political, racial and ethnic lines. Time and again we see the story of Romeo and Juliet play out as love draws fierce rivals together to the chagrin of family. As an emotion, love does not follow logic or reason but rather draws people together based on mystical forces. To this end, love is truly blind. It does not see colour, shape, age or size. It is the source from which all life emanates and one that continually calls its children home. We experience great inner peace when we feel love. The world seems to fall away at the moment we are touched by love.

Acceptance of self and others is at the core of our experience of love. Our protective walls soften, and we are less judgemental when love flows from our being. We actively seek out unconditional love that fully accepts us as we are in any moment. We feel more willing to be our true selves when our loved one is accepting of our uniqueness. In love, our self-judgements seem to drop away and we become more accepting of ourselves. Love quells our critical mind as our focus shifts to joy and happiness. Our spirit is raised up as a result of experiencing love. We notice the sun, the blue sky, the sweet smell of wild roses and the euphoric glow of being in the presence of our beloved. Love brings us into the present moment where time and space seem to disappear into the recesses of our mind. Old wounds heal and new doors appear and open.

When we experience love, our acceptance of others also increases. Our judgements seem small and inconsequential as a result of our elevated focus. We have less interest in the distractions of the world and are more focused on the experience of love. Eknath Easwaran, the Indian born spiritual teacher and author, has written about the need for love to alleviate our distress. He says, "If you do not learn how to love, everywhere you go you are going to suffer."

We are more loving of others when we love and accept ourselves moment to moment. Peace and contentment fill our being when we are loving. When we learn to love ourselves, desire and want drop away like sand through our fingers, as love is all we really need to experience bliss.

Unconditional love is the expression of our divine being. When we experience love we tap into divine consciousness. We are elevated in our awareness and are present to the profoundness of each moment. The dance of atoms, neutrons, protons and electrons is an expression of love. The changing of the seasons is the manifestation of love. Gently touching the hand of our beloved for the first time demonstrates the power of love. Love has such potency as to transform us in an instance, and we can feel like it is the end of the world when we believe love has been taken away.

When we are deeply in touch with our inner love, we feel intoxicated with saturating bliss. We are finally present in the here and now. There are no words to express this, as life simply is. Peace presents itself as if opening like a lotus blossom on the surface of a pond. Just like the lotus blossom, our life is like the journey from the muddy earth, rising up through the murky waters of our consciousness to ultimately reach the clear surface where we can bloom into the glorious expression of love. Love is always within us, whether we feel it or not. It is only when we turn toward it that we awaken to its presence. Just like a mother's love for her child, always present and unconditional, love calls us home to reside in peace and contentment. Love is beyond the mind. It cannot be seen, touched or heard. It can only be experienced, beyond our ability to conceptually understand it. Yet, when we experience it, we are enriched and reminded of our true nature of love, peace and joy.

When we approach life with the perspective of loving compassion, we hold a soft presence that sees life with openness, curiosity and acceptance. We see our reflection in everything and everyone, presenting a world of splendor, as well as revealing areas of unconsciousness that still remain to be transformed. Our judgemental mind, desires and passions hold less weight in the presence of unconditional love. Experiencing love, we are more generous, giving and compassionate toward others and ourselves. Our identification with self transforms from a dualistic perspective to non-dualistic. The ego self fades into the background and our bliss is found in giving to our beloved. When we are presented with challenging situations or people, we can first ask ourselves what the most loving and compassionate action would be to transmute our world into a more blissful place.

Sometimes the greatest act of love can be to call out unconsciousness with the swiftness of an arrow. Love does not mean we indulge in unconscious acts in our world. Rather, true love calls out ignorance with the greatest of compassion in order to raise awareness of our impact. In the workplace, approaching colleagues with kindness and empathy in our hearts can transform the most difficult situations. Being present and affectionate toward our children in good and troubled times demonstrates our love. With our beloved, listening with an open heart, caring and always treating them with kindness nurtures deeper experiences of love. When our world is based on a perspective of love, compassion and kindness, we experience peace, bliss and tranquility in every moment. Love is where we come from, what we want in this human experience and where we are going. It is the elixir of peace and bliss that is always present whenever we turn towards it. Unconditional love embraces the dance of dynamic peace as the expression of the divine in each and every moment.

Having looked at the various ways to remove the barriers to experiencing greater peace, we can next turn to exploring the impact a more peaceful presence has in the world.

Practical application

To apply what you have learned in this section, try one or two of the suggestions below. Take a step, test the water or jump in with both feet. The choice is yours.

Take a step:

- Reflect on the impact that the feeling of love has on you. Notice when you feel more or less loving.
- Observe how the external world seems to soften or disappear when we experience feelings of love.

Test the water:

- When you feel love, consider where it originates from. Is it internal or external to you? How is the experience of love different from the feeling of love?
- Reflect on whether you feel unconditional love from anyone or in any moment. Do you include loving yourself in these moments?

Jump in with both feet:

- Express, more often, the love you feel toward your family, spouse, children, friends and colleagues.
- When you are angry or frustrated with someone, consider what would be the most loving and compassionate response to them. Then respond from this loving perspective. What is your impact?

Chapter Six: The ripple effects of peace

Know the Power that is Peace.

~ Black Elk

The pebble in the pond

> *Better than knowledge is meditation.*
> *But better still is surrender of attachment to results,*
> *because there follows immediate peace.*
> *~ The Bhagavad Gita*

Our consciousness is like a vast open lake. Below the water lies the depths of our unconscious, with areas that we can clearly see and other areas that are hidden from view. Above the water are the areas of our consciousness that we are aware of: our thoughts, feelings and beliefs that create the structure of our life. When we are at peace, the lake is placid with beautiful reflections of the surrounding mountains, trees and the sky. During storms, the water is choppy, churning below the surface, disturbing the bottom sediment, making it murky and unclear. So too, our consciousness can be as peaceful as a calm lake or as disturbed and cloudy as stormy waters.

When we are at peace within ourselves, our inner peace is undisturbed by the blustery waves of life. We may see, hear and feel the turbulence but remain anchored in the quiet witnessing of life as it unfolds with conscious awareness. The impact of our inner peace is like a pebble that has been dropped into a pond. Its ripple affect sends waves of tranquility throughout the vast consciousness, eventually reaching the shoreline and changing its shape, ever so slightly, for all time. At the same time, we are but a drop in the vast ocean of humankind's consciousness. Yet, we still have the ability to influence and impact all the other drops in the ocean with our peaceful conscious awareness. While a pebble or drop may seem small in comparison to the vastness of collective consciousness, our peaceful presence has the ability to evoke greater stillness in the collective consciousness.

In moments of inner peace, we are aware of a state of being that is calm, tranquil and present. Our focus is on the experience of peace that we feel within. Through the ever-changing landscape of life, we are aware that peace is dynamic and that it fluctuates as we go through life's journeys. It seems easier to be at peace when life is unfolding how we believe it should be; we have the relationship we want, or the job we have dreamed of or our health is good. There is a recognition that we have manifested those things that bring us joy.

During challenging times, it seems we can quickly lose our inner sense of peace. Our relationship ends, we do not get the promotion at work or we experience health issues that cause us anxiety and pain. Inner peace creates the ability for us to ride the waves of life while remaining moored in the present moment. Being grounded in inner peace, we see our critical mind, desires and passions while simultaneously remaining detached from their push and pull.

Peace is not a goal to be achieved. Rather it is the outcome of being able to accept what is without judgement, commentary or criticism. Inner peace is a state of being. It is a practice, a meditation, in which we see the upheavals and joys in our life yet remain the detached witness to whatever is unfolding. It arises out of our experiential understanding that we are merely observers of life.

Our inner peace and harmony are disrupted whenever we mistakenly believe we are in control. Fear is the basis of our need to be in control. We try to manage life so that its impact on us is softened or that we get what we believe we want. Fear and peace cannot exist at the same time. Peace can only be experienced when we relinquish control and reside in witness consciousness.

Our greatest impact on others and on the world occurs when we come from a place of inner peace. Our peaceful consciousness is the pebble that we drop into the pond of humanity. Our presence radiates contentment outward like a gentle current shaping the shoreline. Each of us has the ability to be a beacon of peace and kindness in the world through our presence and actions. When we continually work on raising our consciousness by being self-reflective, seeking to understand and being non-judgemental, our world shifts to reflect our own growing inner contentment.

Creating inner peace is a gift that we give not only to ourselves but to the world. We become a calming presence in our workplace, our home, our community and within the global consciousness. We cannot underestimate the impact our presence has in the world by either adding to the struggle and conflict or being a lighthouse of peace and acceptance. By courageously being willing to look at and work through our self-deprecation and judgement, we allow ourselves to deepen our sense of inner peace. Approaching life peacefully and compassionately opens doors for others to create greater peace in their lives. Consistently being in a more peaceful and harmonious state not only influences those who are closest to us but exponentially impacts others in spheres on spheres of influence that we can see and that are also invisible to us.

Consider the impression of someone like Martin Luther King Jr. on his own country, people and the world, or the influence of Mahatma Gandhi's non-violent political actions on the building of a nation, or the impact of Nelson Mandela on the formation of a country previously divided were immense. One person has the potential to affect hundreds, thousands and millions of people through their presence and actions. There can be no greater gift to others than finding our own truth and living that truth in a way that fosters inner peace and contentment. For many of us, our intention may not be to have a global impact but each of us has the potential to influence those around us simply by living a life that fosters greater inner peace and contentment.

Living in a state of inner peace raises the collective consciousness of humankind through the sharing of our presence. Our consciousness is added into the collective, altering its composition and creating new possibilities, where there were previously none. Each of us is drawn toward our true nature, peace and bliss. When we bring contentment to the consciousness of mankind, we remind and shape the collective thinking from an ego gratification state to greater compassion and love for others. Consider how an unselfish act of kindness lifts the spirit of the giver, the receiver and the observer. When we help another human being, we are not only showing them compassion and kindness but also elevating the broader consciousness of mankind through our peaceful actions. Fostering inner peace, we become an example to the world of how to create greater contentment. True happiness is not found in dominance over others or the acquisition of great wealth and power. These are empty conquests compared to the joy, bliss and peace found in treating other beings with compassion, acceptance and love. One of the greatest contributions we can give to the world is the gift of our inner peace. If more of us focused on fostering our own inner peace, the world would be a much more peaceful, accepting and loving place.

Practical application

To apply what you have learned in this section, try one or two of the suggestions below. Take a step, test the water or jump in with both feet. The choice is yours.

Take a step:

- Consider what you believe you have control of in your life (e.g. relationships, health, job, home, community or global events). Now consider what you really have control over?

- Who are the peaceful people in your life or global figures that inspire you? What is it about their way of being that you are drawn to?

Test the water:

- Observe how life is dynamic and ever changing. Notice moments when you are at peace and when your inner peace has dissipated. What are you learning about yourself?

- Notice the impact you have on others and the world when you come from a place of peace. Consciously choose to be a pebble of peace within your own world.

Jump in with both feet:

- Courageously look at your critical mind and let go of daily judgements.

- Consider daily what you are contributing to in your life, work, community and globally. Is your contribution what you aspire it to be? Do something weekly that contributes to peace and compassion.

The Present moment

> *We can never obtain peace in the outer world*
> *until we make peace with ourselves.*
> *~ HH Dalai Lama*

Nurturing inner peace is in service of our highest good. Our capacity to fully experience life expands, and we are less influenced by the distractions of life. By living a more harmonious life we are developing our mind, enhancing our physical well being and strengthening our connection to spirit. We are better able to remain true to our life purpose and path, enabling us to live more in the present moment than being drawn into the past or future. There is greater joy and contentment in our life, and we increasingly accept what is with grace and humility. As a result of experiencing greater inner peace, we begin to recognize a reverence for life, and the profound bliss that is found in the present moment. Inner peace is the by-product of our courageous willingness to look in the mirror, see ourselves truthfully (warts and all) and still love ourselves unconditionally.

When we are committed to continually seeking insight and understanding of our thoughts, feelings and beliefs, inner peace grows, and we experience great harmony and fulfillment in our life. Exploring the mind with an inquisitive and non-judgemental nature unravels our limited thinking to reveal truth beyond our intellect. Our consciousness moves from conceptual understanding to experiential knowing beyond the mind. Slowly our dualistic perspective dissipates and we begin to see our interconnectedness to all phenomenon. As a result, we physically experience more and more moments of stillness and bliss within the body.

While relinquishing our egocentric view of the world can create moments of uneasiness, we also turn toward our discomfort, with a curious nature, to see what is underneath this new revelation. Just like being pulled into a river eddy, we are continually drawn inward by our quest for truth and understanding. Simultaneously, our connection with the divine grows as we reveal ourselves, moment to moment, layer on layer. The more willing we are to really look within, the greater will be our peace and bliss. In these moments, the path in which to serve our highest good is slowly revealed to us and we find peace in its unveiling. Inner peace is the flowering of our true selves where we can be still and fully experience bliss.

Through the journey to inner peace, our life purpose and calling unfolds before our eyes, pointing us in the direction that gives us the greatest joy. At some point in our lives, most of us feel drawn toward a specific life path. We may feel compelled to be a doctor, firefighter, lawyer, business leader, parent, or entrepreneur. Something deep within points us towards a vocation that aligns with our soul's purpose. As we consciously explore deeper aspects of ourselves, our focus shifts away from self-actualization to self-realization, increasing compassion and kindness for ourselves and all beings. Perhaps you are called to be the most conscious leader you can be. Maybe your life purpose is to be a parent who raises conscious children who, in turn, care for others, the environment and the planet. Possibly you feel compelled to be a doctor who sees the humanity in each patient and is filled with understanding and compassion.

When we begin to look deeper into ourselves with conscious awareness, our focus shifts from performing a task to "Who am I being?" As I mentioned earlier, there is a profound difference between doing and *being*. Doing is action-oriented while *being* is about conscious awareness. Today's world is predominantly focused on doing, and seldom gives credence to the importance of simply *being*. When we combine doing and *being*, we experience conscious action, and that carries far greater weight and impact than just going about our lives unconsciously.

Recall that the interplay between being and doing is the dance of dynamic peace. When we allow ourselves to include *being*, our life purpose opens to be more inclusive of all phenomenon rather than being self-absorbed. We realize and see the value in elevating our consciousness to look at our impact beyond ourselves. When we are at peace, there is greater possibility of living a life that is not only the right path for us but also is based on our right livelihood. A life that is full of compassion causes no harm and is ethically positive.[65] The journey toward inner peace is the doorway to self-discovery and contentment.

The road to inner peace is filled with lessons of self-acceptance and courage. The challenges of life, again and again, pull us back into the present moment like the gravitational force of the sun pulling us through space. Inner peace does not protect us from the trials of everyday living, but instead allows us to bend like the willow blowing in the wind. Our roots are deep into the earth and yet we can sway with the winds of change.

Repeatedly we are called to be present, to see ourselves just as we are and in doing so learn to love and accept

---

[65] The Buddhist Centre, Structure/Right Livelihood https://thebuddhistcentre.com/text/right-livelihood

ourselves unabashedly. The insights of each new challenge build on the previous lessons, our ego softens and we grow to see divine nature at play. In my own life, learning to accept and move through periods of self-pity has helped me find greater inner peace. Recognizing my habitual self-denigrating patterns shows me again and again the joy of living a more peaceful life.

Each of us has had moments when we understand why something has happened after the event. Or we keep making the same life choices knowing it is the wrong decision, but we just do not feel we have learned the lesson. Life is about learning to be at peace with what is so that we can love and be loved and eventually know that we are love. What more could one want than living in the experience of love and peace, moment to moment?

Practical application

To apply what you have learned in this section, try one or two of the suggestions below. Take a step, test the water or jump in with both feet. The choice is yours.

Take a step:

- Notice times when you hold a self-centered perspective of the world. From this perspective, what is your level of happiness and peace?

- How peaceful do you feel when your thoughts are of the past? How peaceful do you feel when your thoughts are of the future? How peaceful do you feel when your thoughts are in the present moment?

Test the water:

- What actions are called forth when you are in a state of peaceful reflection? Commit to one action and follow through.

- Observe the difference between doing (taking action) and being (conscious awareness). Do you have a tendency to one state over another? Commit to acting in a way that creates a balance between doing and being.

Jump in with both feet:

- Commit to the ongoing exploration of self in order to experientially know the true meaning of life. Reflect on your actions and motivation, read about concepts of higher thought, meditate regularly, and surround yourself with like-minded people and community.

- Through your self exploration, what are you realizing about yourself? How do these new insights influence you moving forward? Commit to your ongoing development of inner peace.

Family

> *The sage puts himself last and*
> *finds himself in the foremost place.*
> *~Lao-Tzu*

Just like the ripple effects of a pebble dropped into a pond, our peaceful presence within our home and amongst family members engenders a more joyous and tranquil existence day to day. When we are more at peace, there is greater contentment in our homes. We are able to remain more present and accepting of our family members, along with their choices and struggles. Living with greater contentment and joy, we model for our children a way of life that brings about inner peace while promoting acceptance and compassion for all life. By living and modeling inner peace, we are creating the best environment for our family to live a life that is happy and fulfilling. At the same time, one of our greatest challenges to inner peace is letting go of our expectations and desires for our children. As a parent we guide, nurture and care for our children. Yet, we must let them experience the highs and lows of life fully, while always being present in the background should they need our love and support. When we think of family it is typically to reflect on our nuclear family. However, we are all family members of humankind and, more broadly thinking, we are members of the family of living beings on Planet Earth. When we have peace and compassion in our hearts, we understand the sacredness of all life. Living a life that is based on inner peace brings greater joy and contentment to all beings.

Our homes emulate our inner peace as we create greater contentment and joy in our life. The presence that we have within our homes can either increase or decrease tension and stress. When we are calmer and more blissful, our homes mirror our peaceful presence. We become a quieting presence within our home environment. The degree to which there is stillness in our minds is reflected in the tranquility present in our homes. How we choose to create our inner sanctum reflects our state of inner peace. Perhaps you have a place or room in your home that is kept quiet and serene where you regularly return to experience greater stillness. Maybe you have an acreage you walk through daily. Possibly you choose paint colours and furnishings that are soft and inviting. For many, the home is a sanctuary and an oasis that we return to in order to refresh and cleanse our souls from the challenges of life. Fostering a home base that mirrors our commitment to developing inner peace becomes a reminder for all who enter of the power of living a life in contentment and serenity.

The presence we have within our homes has a direct impact on our family members. Being at peace within ourselves creates space for greater acceptance, stillness and calm amongst our family. Our peaceful nature promotes an environment where our spouse and children feel accepted and loved. When a family member is struggling, they will intuitively turn to us for our calming presence and our openness in sharing and discussing whatever is going on for them. When we are at peace within ourselves, people are naturally drawn to us.

Consider a situation where you walk into a room and you can feel the tension and anger. It is typically not a place we would want to stay in for a long time. Now consider a space that is calm, peaceful and serene. We feel welcomed, relaxed and safe in this type of environment. A peaceful presence in our homes can be an anchor that our family members repeatedly return to for comfort, serenity and to be recharged. Living a life that is rewarding and fulfilling models the way for our families. They see and feel our grounded and self-reflective nature and the benefits it has on our life. Our spouse feels supported in finding greater enjoyment in life. Our children learn to make choices that are in service of their highest good. When we are happy and content, we know our families have a greater chance of living a happy life.

As a parent, one of our greatest opportunities is learning the dance of dynamic peace while raising our children. There is a special relationship that we form with our children from birth. We nurture and nourish them from their precious infancy all the way through into adulthood. They are always our children, regardless of their age. As such, we want to protect them from the hardships of life. Our safeguarding can pull us away from our sense of inner peace and contentment. Yet, trying to protect them from the challenges and lessons offered by life would rob them of their own journey to finding inner peace. The opportunity for us as parents is to observe our own worries, fears and expectations for our children and still learn to be at peace within ourselves. When they fall and hurt themselves learning to ride a bike, we can see them learn from their frustrations and feel the exhilaration of mastery. In their struggles with relationships, we can see life's magnificence in helping them to learn self-love. As they leave to go off to university and become adults, we see our ultimate lesson of letting go as if releasing a precious flower into a flowing river. There is a selflessness in caring for our children. We give everything we have to ensure their success and yet we must remain detached. We hold no ownership of our children and yet maintain a responsibility to care for and unconditionally love them. Parenting children gives the gift of learning unconditional love, detachment from our most precious treasurers and ultimate lessons in finding inner peace. When we are at peace, we also provide a great gift to our children: the gift of our peaceful presence, kindness and love.

Our family is more than just our parents, spouse and children. We belong to the family of humankind and ultimately to the family of all beings on this planet we call home. Using DNA, scientists have traced our human interconnectedness back some 60,000 years to East Africa.[66] Despite our different appearances, cultural diversity and artificial nationalistic borders we are all part of the human family. When we live a life that is peaceful, our presence has a calming effect on all humankind.

We are so often inspired by people who model peace and live in a way that does not cause harm. Individuals like Mahatma Gandhi, Ellen Johnson Sirleaf, Jody Williams and HH Dalai Lama have all have had tremendous impact in the world, and they have all been people of peace. Living a life of contentment and joy sends waves of peace out into the vast consciousness of all human beings. We may not all be world leaders of peace, but we can influence one person, our families and our friends who, in turn, influence others to live a life based on a peaceful existence.

In the same way, we are also part of the collective of beings on Mother Earth. The animals, plants, insects and even the earth itself are all living beings. We cannot be fully at peace within ourselves while causing harm to other

---

[66] Fantastic Africa, The Origins of Mankind: Genetics, Andrew Keet, May 25, 2013 https://www.fantasticafrica.org/the-origin-of-mankind-genetics/#.W9NNrfjQbIU

beings. Treating all life as sacred and acting with kindness and compassion toward all beings engenders peace and tranquility within our being. A reverence for all life fosters inner peace and joy.

Practical application

To apply what you have learned in this section, try one or two of the suggestions below. Take a step, test the water or jump in with both feet. The choice is yours.

Take a step:

- Consider what is the right balance of exercising parental control and approaching parenting from a place of witnessing. What are the gifts offered by your children? What gifts do you selflessly give to your children?

- Consider the role you play in bringing joy and peace to all beings. What action could you take differently to foster greater peace and harmony?

Test the water:

- Consider how peaceful your home environment is. How much does your home environment reflect your inner state of peace and calm? Work to create a more peaceful home environment.

- Be present for a family member who is struggling or feels challenged. What is the space you want to create for them, so they feel heard and listened to?

Jump in with both feet:

- Create a space of peace and tranquility in your home for all family members to share. Treat this as a sacred space, meditate there regularly, place a few special objects or treasures in your space, add flowers into your space often.

- What is one thing you can do to bring greater peace to your broader family of beings? What will it take for you to implement this action? Take one step to bring greater peace to other beings.

Community

When we come in contact with one who is inspiring, radiant, and spiritual, those same qualities rise up in us.
~Paramananda

Living a more harmonious life has positive implications on our workplace and broader community. When we have a greater sense of peace within ourselves, we give rise to greater consciousness in the workplace and compassion amongst our work colleagues. Simply by living a peaceful life we unintentionally become a role model for conscious living. Our mindful choices and conscious actions have a ripple effect into our work environments and the neighbourhoods in which we live. Other people begin to view us as having a calming and grounding presence within the turbulence of life. As we continue to pull back the layers of our own unconsciousness, we may even find ourselves to be a voice for compassion and kind-heartedness within our social circles. Fostering greater inner peace and contentment benefits us, as well as the broader communities that we are apart of.

As we continually develop our own sense of inner contentment and harmony, our calming presence can become a refuge in today's stressful and challenging workplace. The pressures of our job can be lessened as a result of creating inner peace. We are better able to be detached from the demands of our job and see things from a broader perspective. We more easily remain grounded in what is truly important to us and less swayed by others' expectations.

Through a regular meditative practice, we become more single-focused, thereby increasing our overall productivity. We are less pulled by the fractured energy of multitasking but more grounded in being present to the task at hand. Our colleagues see us as a person who is calming and approachable. When we participate in work meetings, we bring a sense of balance and openness that can ease tensions. Often, we are seen as an equanimous team member that others come to for advice and support. As we continually look into our own areas of unconsciousness, others begin to view us as having wisdom and good judgement. Our presence may seem extraordinary to others; yet, our gift to the workplace is simply one of being present, non-judgemental and open to whatever is unfolding. In practical terms, our inner peace continues to be the dynamic dance of observing our thoughts, feelings and beliefs with conscious awareness and curiosity. What makes our presence extraordinary is the willingness to return again and again in the exploration for experiential understanding of truth. This self-reflective quality is rare in today's workplace of achieving results and always doing more. For so many people, there is a sense of being on a never-ending treadmill of meeting other people's expectations and always delivering more. When we have a greater sense of peace within ourselves, we are less concerned with what others want and are more focused on remaining true to our own life compass. Inner peace is our lighthouse that guides us safely to the shores of our greatest happiness and joy.

By nurturing inner peace, we spread peace and joy in the communities we live in. The peaceful way in which we live creates a vortex of peace and tranquility. Consider the impact a neighbour has who is disruptive and intrusive. Now reflect on a neighbour who is peaceful, calm and approachable. A presence of peace and compassion within a community is very different from one that is egocentric, confrontational and disruptive. The impact that one person can have on others in their community can be significant. The community events and activities that we support and attend help to shape our communities, such as walking for peace or organizing a meditation for peace. Where we focus our time is a statement of our commitment to a peaceful existence.

When we approach others with kindness and compassion, we create a far different community than when we approach others with hatred and fear. Peace begets peace, kindness fosters acts of kindness and compassion leads to understanding. We also have the opportunity to influence others within our community as a result of our actions and lifestyle choices. By being a voice for peaceful co-habitation with all beings, we can change attitudes, perspectives and laws to be more inclusive, tolerant and kind. Our very presence and way of being in the world speaks volumes to those around us. We are and always will be interconnected with all beings. Living in peace and contentment sends shock waves of bliss out into the collective consciousness of our communities.

Our actions and deeds speak far more than words. When we regularly sit to meditate, we are not only recalibrating and slowing ourselves down, but we are also doing the same for all those around us. Energetically we shift all consciousness through our committed action. Just as the world is a mirror for us, we too are a reflection in the mirror. We return back to the world our contentment and joy, which is then mirrored back to us. This cycle of reflection, insight, integration and mirroring back continues until eventually we have merged subject (ourselves) and object (the external world). Our sense of self has united with all manifest phenomenon, and we have become one with all and everything. Similarly, when our actions are based on a sense of inner peace and happiness, there is less craving, desire or want. Our actions are founded in compassion, kindness and love. We give freely without attachment to the outcome. Consider the unconditional love for a newborn child, the random acts of kindness toward strangers or the selfless act to alleviate someone's suffering. We are more present for these moments when we have unveiled our own areas of unconsciousness. Finding a sense of inner peace lifts our own suffering and in turn allows us to be a beacon for others.

Practical application

To apply what you have learned in this section, try one or two of the suggestions below. Take a step, test the water or jump in with both feet. The choice is yours.

Take a step:

- Consider how your work colleagues view you in the workplace. Are you having the desired peaceful impact you want to have?

- What type of neighbour are you? Are you contributing to the collective happiness in your community or adding to the disharmony?

Test the water:

- Notice the degree of peace and harmony within the workplace. What can you do to creates great contentment and joy? Do one thing to create greater peace in your workplace.

- What is your presence within your community? Do you add to the enrichment of the collective consciousness or do you create disharmony and unrest? Take one action to increase peace within your community.

Jump in with both feet:

- Meditate regularly on peace and harmony in your community.

- Participate in a community event that promotes peace, tolerance and compassion for all beings.

Global

> *If we have no peace,*
> *it is because we have forgotten*
> *that we belong to each other.*
> *~ Mother Teresa*

World peace begins with each of us. When we are at peace within ourselves our world is peaceful. We bring our harmonious existence into the world and add to the peaceful presence of other beings. Our combined energy is like a thousand bright stars in the vastness of dark space. Through a peaceful existence, we become beacons of light in the consciousness of humankind. There are many challenges to remaining peaceful, particularly during times of conflict and war. Yet, even in dark times, there are always those beings of kindness and compassion who stand out against the backdrop of tyranny. Solving world peace can only be accomplished by first finding peace within ourselves. Only when we have peace in our hearts can we hope to solve the challenges of the world. We must see our interconnectedness and interdependence rather than our distinctiveness. The suffering of other beings is our suffering. The joy and happiness of others is our joy and happiness. When we treat others with kindness and compassion the whole world is elevated. Our responsibility to humankind is to find inner peace within ourselves so all beings can find it in themselves.

We cannot offer to others what we do not have to give. In order to share peace, we first must find it within ourselves. We must nurture our own sense of self-acceptance and inner contentment before we can expect to be of service to our family, friends, community and ultimately humankind. So much of the hatred and oppression in the world has been the result of self-denigration and self-hatred. When this self-denigration is carried out to the extremes, we have seen acts of narcissism, ethnocentrism and genocide. When we learn to love and accept ourselves, inner peace naturally occurs within us, and we then have a greater capacity for kindness and compassion toward others. Through ongoing reflection and acceptance of our own perceived imperfections, we develop the ability to be more accepting of others. We see within others our own struggles and trials.

When we see others judging and chastising themselves, our own self-denigration is reflected back to us. Seeing the suffering arising out of a stormy relationship, we are reminded of our own periods of suffering. Watching the torment of losing a loved one, we feel the pain that surfaced at a time of our own loss. As we find greater inner peace through the experiences of our own suffering, our hearts open toward the suffering of all living beings. The more grounded we are in the dance of dynamic peace, the greater is the well from which we can draw compassion, wisdom and kindness for others.

It can be challenging to be at peace during times of global upheaval and conflict. The ravages of war, the violent acts of terrorists, the tyranny of governments and the brutality of gangs cause us to question whether peace is possible, or if it is just a utopian dream. Yet for all the darkness in the world, there is an equal proportion of light. While the balance may seem polarized, to one extreme over the other, there is always a matching force at play. We have seen examples of this throughout history and even in today's current events: the White Helmets of the Syrian Civil War, are ordinary citizens who rush into conflict to save lives; the men and women during World War II who hid and protected people of Jewish decent; vigils held across Canada and New Zealand in response to a shooting in a Mosque; Americans of all faiths coming together at a Synagogue to protect the Jewish congregation. There are many examples of individuals, groups and nations that have come to the aid of their fellow human beings. Without compassion in their hearts and a willingness to stand up for the suffering of others, these acts of kindness would not occur. This is why it is so important for each of us to find peace in our lives.

The peace we hold within our being is extended out into the world. If just ten percent of the 2018 global population of 7.6 billion people focused or meditated on world peace, imagine the impact it would have on the rest of humanity. Thus, world peace begins with each of us, moment to moment, creating greater peace in our lives and sharing that peace amongst our family, friends, communities and ultimately the world.

We must recognize our interconnectedness and interdependence with each other. What happens in one part of the world has a direct impact on the rest of the planet. The effects of global deforestation, melting glaciers, pollution, nuclear waste, economic markets and political change all have an impact on life on our planet. What happens in one part of the world has a direct bearing on others around the world. As we know, our interconnectedness is not limited to the use of technology or global warming but also our molecular connection down to the smallest of particles. The air we breathe is the same air breathed by others on the opposite side of the planet. The energy that flows through your body is the same energy flowing through everyone and every living being. Our thoughts, feelings and beliefs are shared not just verbally but also energetically. We cannot separate ourselves from the vast consciousness of humankind.

Each of us may feel like a drop in the ocean of consciousness but we are part of a collective consciousness of humanity. We are changed by others and can bring about change through our presence. When we begin to see the happiness of others is impacting our own happiness, only then can we begin to create peace around the world. In the same way, the suffering of others is a reflection of our own suffering. When we harm another living being, we are harming ourselves. The destruction of life is ultimately destroying our own life. Only through the realization of inner peace, compassion and a reverence for all life, can we hope to begin to create peace on this planet we call home. Our responsibility is to find peace within ourselves so we can add to the contentment and harmony around the world. Our duty is to not cause harm to ourselves or any living being. To do so only proliferates ongoing suffering in the world. When we treat ourselves, other human beings, animals, plants and the earth with gentleness, compassion and kindness, we will be spreading peace around the world.

Practical application

To apply what you have learned in this section, try one or two of the suggestions below. Take a step, test the water or jump in with both feet. The choice is yours.

Take a step:

- Consider how your own self-negation impacts family, friends and ultimately the broader collective consciousness. In what way can you contribute to greater peace and joy?
- Recognize our interconnectedness and interdependence. What's one action you can take to

care for the people, community and/or environment around you?

Test the water:

- Meditate on world peace daily, weekly or monthly.
- What are some examples, that you know of, of people caring for other beings in the world? Join a global cause for peace.

Jump in with both feet:

- Participate in a global meditation practice.
- Become a voice for peace and compassion in the world.

Chapter Seven: Looking forward

Our lives are a continual journey of self-discovery. When we purposefully pursue living with conscious awareness and compassion for all beings, we experience greater fulfillment and inner peace. True happiness surfaces when we step out of our egocentrism and focus on the happiness of all beings. Living a life that creates a peaceful existence not only lifts our spirits but also the spirit of those around us. We must be willing to ask ourselves, "Are we adding to the stress and unhappiness in the world or being a beacon of light for others to find their way home to inner peace?"

With so much suffering and dissatisfaction in our communities and around the world, your light is needed like a lighthouse to a safe harbour of peace and contentment. Peace will always be found, first and foremost, from within. This peace is found in being able to be present with oneself, by not causing harm and by honouring life. The profound peace found in the full experience of the present moment is the peace of a still and present mind. The dance of dynamic peace is the journey to true freedom.

My challenge to you in moving forward is to consider the following suggested steps to living a more peaceful and harmonious life:

1. Commit to finding greater peace and contentment within your life.

2. Have an unwavering personal pursuit to live a life that is fulfilling and full of joy, happiness and peace.

3. Look to see our interconnectedness and interdependence in all life.

4. Be a champion for the rights and protection of all living beings, including Mother Earth.

5. As my root teacher would say, "Meditate, meditate, meditate."

May your days be spent in the eternal present moment where peace, joy and love await your return home.

Acknowledgements

To Ann Brindle for her gift of enlightening quotes.

To Nick Kettles for his on-going coaching support and encouragement to just write, and for graciously agreeing to edit my book.

To Natasha Lyndon for being the first to read and proofread my manuscript.

To my best friend, Andrea Earle, for taking the time to read my book and provide her invaluable feedback and encouragement.

To all my teachers throughout my life who have influenced me immeasurably, in particular, Master Charles Cannon, Pema Chodron, Thich Nhat Hanh and the Venerable Gawa Khandro.

To my partner Paul for his never-ending love, support and encouragement.

Appendix A – Personal Values Exercise

Below is a list of values commonly used in helping people discover their personal core values. This list is not exhaustive, but it will give you an idea of some common core values. If there are words that better align to your core values, please include them.

Steps:

1. Circle all of the values in the list below that resonate with you (or add your own if you wish).
2. Pick your top ten.
3. Narrow the list to your top five.
4. Rank your top five in order of their importance.
5. Consider whether your life is in alignment with your top five values. If not, make changes to be in better alignment. This will lead you to a more fulfilling and rewarding life.

Accountability	Citizenship
Accuracy	Collaboration
Achievement	Comfort
Adaptability	Commitment
Adventurous	Community
Altruistic	Compassion
Approachable	Competency
Authenticity	Competitive
Authority	Confidentiality
Autonomy	Contentment
Balance	Contribution
Beauty	Control
Belonging	Courage
Boldness	Creativity
Bravery	Credibility
Calm	Curiosity
Caring	Decisive
Challenge	Dedication

Dependability	Generosity
Determination	Goodness
Devotion	Gratitude
Dignity	Growth
Duty	Happiness
Efficient	Harmony
Empathy	Health
Encouragement	Helpful
Equanimity	Honesty
Fairness	Humble
Faith	Humility
Fame	Humor
Family	Imagination
Fearless	Impartial
Fidelity	Independence
Focus	Individuality
Friendships	Influence
Fun	Inner Harmony

Innovation	Mystery
Inspiration	Openness
Integrity	Optimism
Irreverence	Order
Joy	Organization
Justice	Partnership
Kindness	Passion
Knowledge	Patience
Leadership	Peace
Learning	People
Longevity	Perseverance
Love	Persuasive
Loyalty	Philanthropic
Mastery	Play
Maturity	Pleasure
Meaningful	Poise
Mindful	Popularity
Motivation	Positive

Power	Resourceful
Practical	Respect
Precise	Responsibility
Pride	Reverence
Privacy	Risk taking
Professionalism	Rule of law
Punctuality	Sacrifice
Purity	Safety
Rational	Security
Realistic	Self-Awareness
Recognition	Self-Control
Reflection	Selflessness
Relationships	Self-Respect
Relaxation	Sense of humor
Reliability	Serenity
Religion	Service
Reputation	Solitude
Resilience	Spirituality

Stability

Status

Strength

Success

Sympathy

Thoughtfulness

Tranquility

Transparency

Trustworthiness

Truth

Useful

Valor

Virtue

Wealth

Wisdom

Made in the USA
Middletown, DE
19 August 2019